CELEBRATING OUR FAMILIES

CRAFTS FOR KIDS

Compiled by Linda Crisp

Gospel Light

How to make clean copies from this book.

You may make copies of portions of this book with a clean conscience if:

✦ you (or someone in your organization) are the original purchaser;

✦ you are using the copies you make for a noncommercial purpose
  (such as teaching or promoting a ministry) within your church or organization;

✦ you follow the instructions provided in this book.

However, it is illegal for you to make copies if:

✦ you are using the material to promote, advertise or sell a product
  or service other than for ministry fund-raising;

✦ you are using the material in or on a product for sale;

✦ you or your organization are not the original purchaser of this book.

By following these guidelines you help us keep our products affordable.

Thank you,

Gospel Light

Library of Congress Cataloging-in-Publication Data
Crisp, Linda
    Celebrating our families craft book / compiled by Linda Crisp.
        p.   cm.
    Includes index.
    ISBN 0-8307-1675-0 : $14.99
    1. Handicraft.   I. Title.
TT145.C75   1995
745.5—dc20   94-32091
                                                           CIP

Bill Greig III, Publisher ♦ **Billie Baptiste,** Publisher, Product Research ♦ **Dr. Elmer L. Towns,** Senior Consulting Publisher ♦ **Gary S. Greig, Ph.D.,** Editor in Chief ♦ **Linda Crisp,** Editor ♦ **Christy Weir,** Senior Editor ♦ **Linda Bossoletti,** Editorial Coordinator ♦ **Linda Crisp, Carrie Guzik, Neva Hickerson, Loreen Robertson, Jan Shewmon, Donna Ward,** Contributing Writers ♦ **Sheryl Haystead, Neva Hickerson, Jan Shewmon, Christy Weir, Jan Worsham,** Contributing Editors ♦ **Carolyn Thomas,** Designer ♦ **Chizuko Yasuda,** Illustrator

© 1995 Gospel Light, Ventura, California 93006. All rights reserved. Printed in U.S.A.

Contents

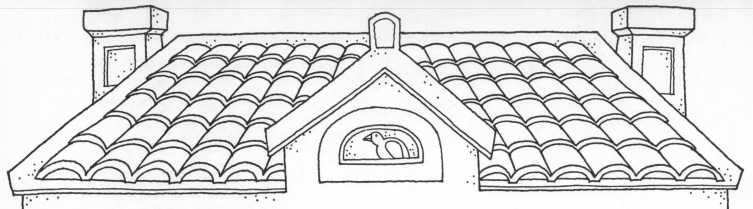

Introduction to Celebrating Our Families Craft Book

Family Fun

God designed families to love each other and build close relationships with one another. However, in the busyness of modern life, families are finding it increasingly difficult to spend meaningful time together. This resource book is designed to bring families together by celebrating the importance of family and home.

In addition to teaching about family life, you will also find a variety of multicultural crafts. Your students will gain a new appreciation for the unique traditions, customs and celebrations that each family possesses.

We hope that you and your students will come to appreciate your own families as you complete projects from *Celebrating Our Families Craft Book.*

Personalize It!

We encourage you to use *Celebrating Our Families Craft Book* as a basis for your craft program. You, as the teacher, parent or craft leader, play an essential role in leading enjoyable and successful craft projects for your children.

Feel free to alter the craft materials and instructions to suit your children's needs. Consider what materials you have on hand, what materials are available in your area and what materials you can afford to purchase. In some cases you will be able to substitute materials to use something you already have.

In addition, don't feel confined to the crafts in a particular age-level section. You may want to adapt a craft for younger and older age levels.

Three Steps to Success

What can you do to make sure craft time is successful and fun for your students?

✦ **First,** encourage creativity in each child! Remember the process of creating is just as important as the final product. Provide a variety of materials with which children may work. Allow children to make choices on their own. Don't expect every child's project to turn out the same. Don't insist that children "stay in the lines."

✦ **Second,** choose projects that are appropriate for the skill level of your students. Children become easily discouraged when a project is too difficult for them. Keep your children's skill level in mind when choosing craft projects. Finding the right projects for your students will increase the likelihood that all will be successful and satisfied with their finished products.

✦ **Finally,** show an interest in the unique way each child approaches a project. Affirm the choices he or she has made. Treat each child's final product as a "masterpiece"!

The comments you give a child today can affect the way he or she views art in the future—so make it positive! Remember—the ability to create is part of being made in the image of God, the Creator!

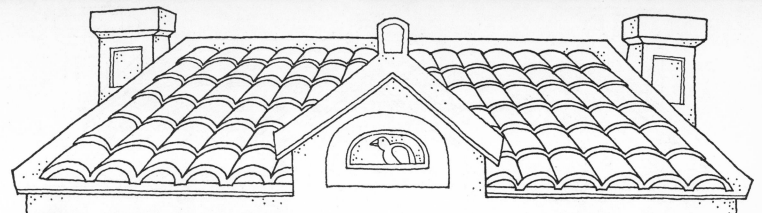

Be Prepared

If you are planning to use crafts with a child at home, here are three helpful tips:

✦ Focus on the crafts in the book designated for your child's age, but don't ignore projects that are listed for older or younger ages. Elementary-age children enjoy many of the projects geared for preschool and kindergarten children. And younger children are always interested in doing "big kid" things. Just plan on working along with the child, helping with tasks the child can't handle alone.

✦ Start with projects that call for materials you have around the house. Make a list of the items you do not have that are needed for projects you think your child will enjoy. Plan to gather those supplies in one expedition.

✦ If certain materials seem too difficult to obtain, a little thought can usually lead to appropriate substitutions. And often the homemade version ends up being an improvement over the original plan.

If you are planning to lead a group of children in doing craft projects, keep these hints in mind:

✦ Choose projects that will allow children to work with a variety of materials.

✦ Make your selection of all projects far enough in advance to allow time to gather all needed supplies in one coordinated effort. Many projects use some of the same items.

✦ Make up a sample of each project to be sure the directions are fully understood and potential problems can be avoided. You may want to adapt some projects to simplify procedures or vary the materials required.

✦ Many items can be acquired as donations from people or businesses if you plan ahead and make your needs known. Many churches distribute lists of materials needed to their congregations and community and are able to provide crafts at little or no cost. Some items can be brought by the children themselves.

✦ In making your supplies list, distinguish between items that every individual child will need and those that will be shared among a group.

✦ Keep in mind that some materials may be shared among more than one age level, but only if there is good coordination between the groups. It is extremely frustrating to a teacher to expect to have scissors, only to discover another group is using them. Basic supplies that are used repeatedly in craft projects should usually be provided to every group.

Family Talk

Each craft in this book includes a very important section entitled "Family Talk." These sections are designed to help you enhance craft times with thought-provoking conversation and are key to relating the project to family life. Each section is geared to encourage your students to share something about their own families. If your crafts program includes large groups of children, you may want to share these conversation suggestions with each helper who can in turn use them with individuals or small groups. You may also want to provide a map for the children to look at when doing multicultural crafts.

Craft Symbols

Many of the craft projects in *Celebrating Our Families Craft Book* are appropriate for more than one age level. Next to the title of certain projects in this book you'll find the symbol shown below. This symbol tells what projects are suitable or adaptable for all elementary-age children—first through sixth grade. As you select projects, consider the particular children you are working with. Feel free to use your own ideas to make projects simpler or more difficult depending on the needs of your students.

In addition, some craft projects in this book require less preparation than others. The symbol shown below tells which projects require minimal preparation.

Helpful Hints

Using Glue with Young Children

Since preschoolers have difficulty using glue bottles effectively, you may want to try one of the following procedures. Purchase glue in large containers (up to one gallon size).

a. Pour small amount of glue into several shallow containers (such as margarine tubs or the bottoms of soda bottles).

b. Dilute glue by mixing a little water into each container.

c. Children use paste brushes to spread glue on project.

OR

a. Pour a small amount of glue into a plastic margarine tub.

b. Give each child a cotton swab. The child dips the cotton swab into the glue and rubs glue on project.

glue level

c. Excess glue can be poured back into the large container at the end of each session.

swabs

Cutting with Scissors

When cutting with scissors is required for these crafts, take note of the fact that some of the children in your class may be left-handed. It is very difficult for a left-handed person to cut with scissors that were designed to be used with the right hand. Have available in your classroom two or three pairs of left-handed scissors. These can be obtained from a school supply center.

Using Acrylic Paints

Acrylic paints are required for many of the wood projects. Our suggestions are:

✦ Provide smocks or old shirts for your children to wear, as acrylics may stain clothes.

✦ Acrylics can be expensive for a large group of children. To make paint go further, squeeze a small amount into a shallow container and add water until mixture has a creamy consistency. Or you may use acrylic house paints.

✦ Fill shallow containers with soapy water. Clean paintbrushes before switching colors and immediately after finishing project.

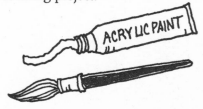

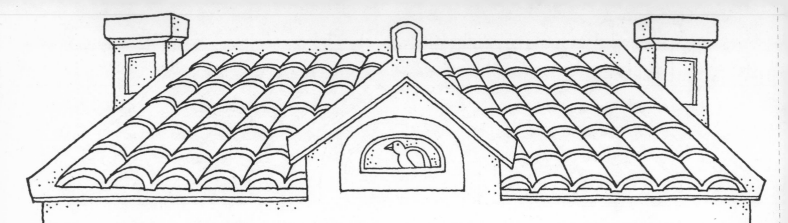

Crafts with a Message

Many of the projects in *Celebrating Our Families Craft Book* can easily become crafts with a message. Children can create slogans or poetry as part of their projects. Or, you may want to provide photocopies of an appropriate poem, thought or Bible verse for children to attach to their crafts. Below are some examples of ways to use verses and drawings to enhance the craft projects in this book.

Section One/Prekindergarten-Kindergarten
Crafts for Young Children

Craft projects for young children are a blend of, "I wanna do it myself!" and "I need help!" Each project, because it is intended to come out looking like a recognizable something, usually requires a certain amount of adult assistance—in preparing a pattern, in doing some cutting, in preselecting magazine pictures, in tying a knot, etc. The younger the child, the more the adult will need to do, but care must always be taken not to rob the child of the satisfaction of his or her own unique efforts. Neither must the adult's desire to have a nice finished project override the child's pleasure at experimenting with color and texture. Avoid the temptation to do the project for the child or to improve on the child's efforts.

Some of the crafts have enrichment and simplification ideas included with them. An enrichment idea provides a way to make the craft more challenging for the older child. A simplification idea helps the younger child complete the craft more successfully. If you find a child frustrated with some of the limitations of working on a structured craft—although most of the projects in this book allow plenty of leeway for children to be themselves—it may be a signal the child needs an opportunity to work with more basic, less structured materials: blank paper and paints, play dough, or abstract collages (gluing miscellaneous shapes or objects onto surfaces such as paper, cardboard or anything else to which glue will adhere). Remember the cardinal rule of thumb in any task a young child undertakes: The process the child goes through is more important than the finished product.

Puzzling Photo Frame

(25-30 MINUTES)

Materials: Acrylic spray paint in a variety of bright colors, poster board, ribbon, stapler and staples, pencil, masking tape, craft glue, scissors, ruler, newspaper. For each child—20 small jigsaw puzzle pieces (they don't need to fit together).

Preparation: In well-ventilated area, cover ground with newspaper and spray paint front of puzzle pieces in a variety of colors. Cut poster board into 4x5-inch (10x12.5-cm) rectangles—two for each child. Cut a 2x3-inch (5x7.5-cm) opening from the center of one rectangle to make a frame (sketch a)—one for each child. Use pencil to draw a line along sides and bottom of frame border as a guide for gluing. Cut ribbon into 12-inch (30-cm) lengths—one for each child.

Instruct each child in the following procedures:

✦ With teacher's help, staple one end of ribbon onto corner of uncut poster board piece. Staple other end of ribbon onto opposite corner to make a hanger (sketch b).

✦ Spread glue along pencil lines around frame (sketch c).

✦ With teacher's help, place uncut poster board piece on top of frame with staples facing in (sketch c).

✦ Overlap and glue puzzle pieces around frame to decorate. Allow glue to dry.

✦ Take frame home. With parent's help, slide a family photograph through top of frame. Hang picture frame.

Simplification Ideas: Omit painting puzzle pieces. Use pasta boxes (the kind with plastic windows) to make front of frame.

Enrichment Ideas: Children use felt pens instead of spray paint to color the back sides of puzzle pieces. Glue a frame stand to back of picture instead of hanging.

Family Talk:

Have you ever put a puzzle together? All the pieces join together to make one picture. Families are like puzzles—each person is a separate piece but when joined together make one whole family. God created our families to stick together, even when times are tough!

Simple Scrapbook Cover

(15-20 MINUTES)

Materials: Sturdy wallpaper in a variety of colors and patterns, rickrack in a variety of colors, hole punch, pencil, glue, scissors, measuring stick. For each child—three brads.

Preparation: Cut wallpaper into 12x19-inch (30x47.5-cm) rectangles—one for each child.

Instruct each child in the following procedures:

✦ Fold wallpaper in half to make book cover.

✦ With teacher's help, punch three evenly spaced holes in left margin of book.

✦ Secure a brad through each hole.

✦ With teacher's help, use pencil to write the initial of your last or first name.

✦ Cut and glue rickrack onto pencil lines.

Enrichment Idea: Use scribble pads or brown paper bags cut into 12x19-inch (30x47.5-cm) sheets for scrapbook pages.

Family Talk:

What is a scrapbook? A scrapbook is a special book with lots of pages. We glue or tape things that we want to save onto the pages so that they don't get lost or damaged. In your scrapbook, you can save pictures, awards, cards, letters or anything else that will help you remember special times you had with your families and friends. When did you have a fun time with your family?

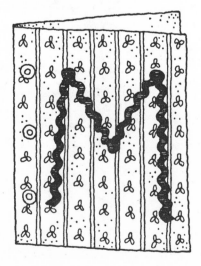

Rock Relatives

(30-40 MINUTES)

Materials: Felt in a variety of bright colors; brown, black, orange, white and yellow yarn; round stones in a variety of shapes and sizes; small wiggle eyes; craft glue; scissors; cotton balls. For each child—a small piece of driftwood.

Instruct each child in the following procedures:

✦ Choose one stone and two wiggle eyes for each family member.

✦ Glue two eyes onto each stone. Allow glue to dry.

✦ With teacher's help, cut and glue yarn and felt on top of each stone to make hair or a hat for each family member.

✦ Glue stones onto piece of driftwood, in nooks and crannies. To secure each stone in place, wedge pieces of cotton into gaps between driftwood and stone.

Simplification Idea: For younger children, glue eyes, yarn, etc. onto one large stone to make one family member.

Enrichment Ideas: Glue small seashells onto tops of stones for hats. Use white correction fluid and permanent black felt pen to draw eyes on pebbles. Glue pieces of moss onto driftwood for further decoration. Brush clear nail polish on pebbles to make them shiny.

Family Talk:

How many people are in your family? Some families are small and some families are large. But God loves every family no matter what size it is. Let's thank God for giving each of us a family!

African Message Pocket

(15-20 MINUTES)

Materials: Yarn or leather lacing, crayons, hole punch, transparent tape, scissors, measuring stick. For each child—one 6x9-inch (15x22.5-cm) manila envelope, four wooden beads.

Preparation: Cut off 2 inches (5 cm) from the top of each manila envelope (sketch a). Punch six evenly spaced holes along both sides of envelope (sketch b). Cut yarn or leather lacing into 4-yard (1.2-m) lengths—one for each child. Wrap a piece of tape around one end of each yarn or leather lacing piece and tie a knot at other end.

Instruct each child in the following procedures:

✦ Use crayons to draw designs or nature scenes on both sides of envelope.

✦ Slide two beads onto yarn or leather lacing piece just above knot (sketch c). Thread yarn through holes on both sides of envelope, leaving a large loop at the top (sketch d). Slide two beads onto remaining end of yarn and, with teacher's help, tie a knot to secure.

✦ Wear Message Pocket on shoulder or attach to belt loops.

Enrichment Idea: Older children can punch own holes in envelopes.

Family Talk:

Optional: Show Africa on a map. **In some parts of Africa people wear traditional clothing that consists of a piece of cloth wrapped around the body. The cloth has no buttons, zippers or pockets. Since they don't have built-in pockets, like our shirts or pants do, they carry pockets. What will you put in your Message Pocket? Write a kind note to a family member and place it in your Message Pocket. Deliver the message to him or her today!**

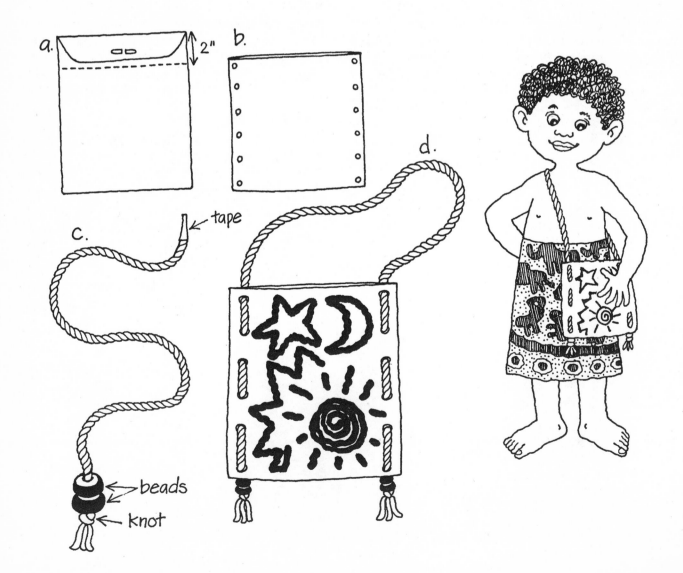

Mexican Cup Catch

(15-20 MINUTES)

Materials: Construction paper in a variety of colors, string, hole punches, felt pens, transparent tape, craft knife, scissors, ruler. For each child—one large orange juice can, one ¾-inch (1.9-cm) wooden bead.

Preparation: Cut off 2¾ inches (6.9 cm) from top of each orange juice can and discard (sketch a). Cut construction paper into 2x9-inch (5x22.5-cm) rectangles—one for each child. Cut string into 12-inch (30-cm) lengths—one for each child. Wrap a piece of tape around one end of each string and tie a knot at other end.

Instruct each child in the following procedures:
♦ Use felt pens to decorate paper.
♦ Wrap paper around can and tape in place.
♦ With teacher's help, punch hole near top edge of can.
♦ Thread bead onto string and slide just above knot. With teacher's help, tie bead to string (sketch b).
♦ Tie opposite end of string through hole (sketch c).
♦ Hold cup and try to toss the bead into the cup.

Enrichment Ideas: Use self-adhesive paper instead of construction paper to cover cup. To make a handle: Glue one end of a 6-inch (15-cm) length of dowel to bottom of cup (sketch d).

Family Talk:

This cup catch game is played by children in Mexico. What kind of games does your family like to play? Do your games have rules? It's fun to play games when everybody obeys the rules of the game. What happens when we don't follow the rules?

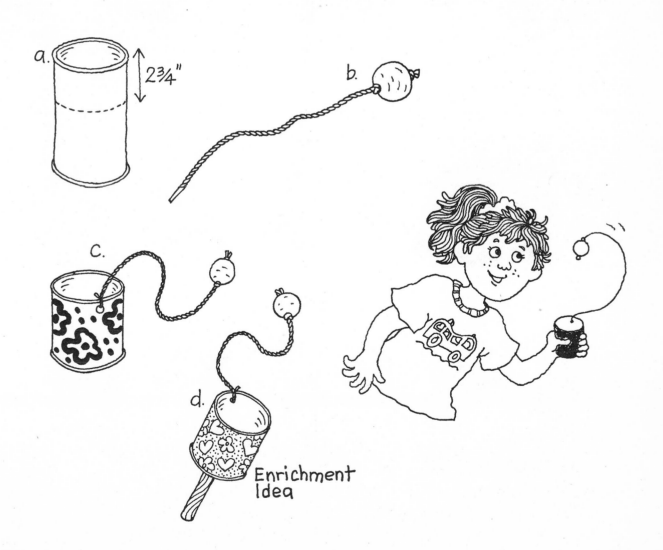

13

Sweeties Jar

(TWO-DAY PROJECT/40-60 MINUTES)

Materials: Rainbow-colored candy sprinkles, flour, salt, water, measuring cup, large bowl, mixing spoon, cookie sheet, small cookie cutters, forks, oven, clear acrylic spray, medium-width ribbon, glue, scissors, measuring stick, newspaper. For each child—one small glass jar with metal lid, one plastic sandwich bag.

Preparation: Make dough. The following recipe will make enough dough for eight children: Mix 4 cups flour, 1 cup salt and 1½ cups water until mixture clings together. Knead mixture on floured surface until smooth. Divide mixture into eight balls and place in individual sandwich bags. Make additional dough for decorations. Cut ribbon into 18-inch (45-cm) lengths—one for each child. Cover outside area with newspaper.

Instruct each child in the following procedures:

DAY ONE:
- ✦ Shape dough ball onto top of jar lid (sketch a).
- ✦ Flatten additional dough on flat surface. Press cookie cutter into dough to make a shape.
- ✦ Moisten bottom of dough shape with water and place on top of dough lid (sketch b).

- ✦ Use fork to poke several holes in dough to allow air to escape when baking.
- ✦ Place dough lids on cookie sheet. Teacher bakes dough at 250 degrees for two to three hours or until dough hardens.

DAY TWO:
- ✦ Glue candy sprinkles or other decorations onto lid.
- ✦ In well-ventilated area, spray jar lid with clear spray and allow to dry (about two minutes).
- ✦ With teacher's help, tie ribbon around rim of jar.
- ✦ Gently screw lid onto jar.
- ✦ Use jar for storage at home.

Enrichment Idea: Paint fun-shaped pasta and glue onto top of dough lid.

Family Talk:

Who in your family cooks the most meals? How do you help out in the kitchen? It's good to help when we're asked. But it's even better when we help our family without being asked. God planned for families to work together and help each other. What will you do today to help someone in your family?

a.

b.

Broken-Up Vase

(25-30 MINUTES)

Materials: Tempera paint in a variety of colors, paint-brushes, shallow containers, glue, newspaper. For each child—one small bottle or jar, approximately six eggshells.

Preparation: Wash eggshells and allow to dry. Pour glue into shallow containers. Pour paint into additional shallow containers. Cover work area with newspaper.

Instruct each child in the following procedures:

✦ On paved area, place eggshells between two sheets of newspaper and stomp on shells to crush them. (Note: Make sure children are wearing shoes.)

✦ Use paintbrush to cover entire bottle or jar with glue.

✦ Remove top sheet of newspaper and roll bottle or jar onto crushed eggshells (sketch a). Allow glue to dry.

✦ Paint vase to decorate. Let dry.

Simplification Idea: Crush eggshells ahead of time.

Family Talk:

We broke eggshells to make our vases. Have you ever broken something in your house and were afraid to tell your mom or dad? When you tell the truth about breaking something, what would you like your (mom) to say or do? How do you feel when someone forgives you? And if somebody breaks one of your toys, you can think about how they might feel. You can ask God to help you to forgive others.

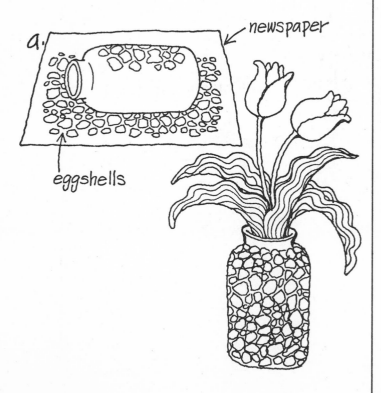

Family Place Mats

(20-25 MINUTES)

Materials: Several magazines with a variety of pictures (showing animals, foods, sports, etc.), poster board in a variety of colors, clear self-adhesive paper, glue sticks, scissors, measuring stick.

Preparations: Cut poster board into 9x12-inch (22.5x30-cm) mats—two for each child. Cut self-adhesive paper into 10x13-inch (25x32.5-cm) rectangles—four for each child. Look through magazines and tear out appropriate pages.

Instruct each child in the following procedures:

✦ Cut out magazine pictures of objects that tell about two family members (such as hobbies, interests, favorite animals, favorite food). Medium-sized pictures work best— 8 to 12 for each family member.

✦ Arrange cutouts for one family member on a poster board mat of his or her favorite color. Lightly glue cutouts in place. Repeat process for second family member.

✦ With teacher's help, peel adhesive backing from clear paper and place on front of place mat. Then, peel adhesive backing from second piece of clear paper and place on back of place mat. Repeat process for second place mat.

✦ With teacher's help, cut edges of self-adhesive paper as close as possible to edges of place mats.

✦ At home, child places place mats on table where the family members sit.

Simplification Idea: On poster board, children draw pictures of objects representing family members.

Enrichment Ideas: Make place mats for additional family members as time allows. Use felt pens or cut out letters to spell out family member's name on place mat.

Family Talk:

What is your (mom's) favorite color? What is your (dad's) favorite food? Each member of your family has different likes and dislikes—that's what makes us special! Your place mats can help you remember how each family member is special. Talking at mealtimes is one way of learning about other family members' interests.

Mexican Bark Painting

(20-25 MINUTES)

Materials: Large brown paper grocery sacks, fluorescent poster paints, shallow containers, black felt pens, scissors, ruler, newspaper. For each child—one cotton swab.

Preparation: Cut grocery sacks into 10x12-inch (25x30-cm) rectangles—one for each child. Turn paper printed side down. Use felt pen to draw a double border along edge of paper (sketch a). Cover work area with newspaper. Pour paint into shallow containers.

Instruct each child in the following procedures:

♦ Use felt pen to draw a family scene inside the border on brown paper.

♦ Crumple picture into a ball as tight as possible. Then open and smooth paper. This makes the paper look like bark.

♦ Dip cotton swab into paint and dab dots inside the border (sketch b). Add touches of paint to color in the picture.

Enrichment Idea: For a more authentic look, dip crumpled paper into a mixture of water and brown tempera paint. Open and smooth paper. Hang to dry before using felt pens or paint. Glue small pieces of bark around edge of paper to create a border. To hang picture: Fold top edge of picture back, place a length of string or yarn inside fold and staple fold shut (sketch c).

Family Talk:

What is paper made from? Trees! In Mexico, people paint pictures on the bark of trees. Optional: Show Mexico on a map. **Do you know anybody from Mexico? Has anyone in your family ever visited Mexico? Mexican artists paint colorful pictures of celebrations and people working and playing in the village. You can make a picture of your family working and playing together!**

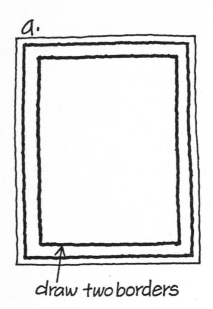

a.

draw two borders

b.

cotton swab

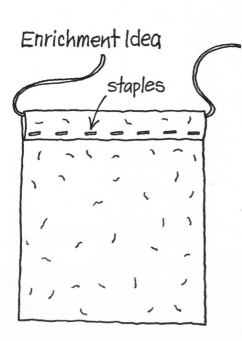

Enrichment Idea

staples

My Own Maracas

(15-20 MINUTES)

Materials: Acrylic paint in a variety of colors, paintbrushes, shallow containers, dried beans, ¼-inch (.625-cm) dowels, saw, knife, glue, ruler, newspaper. For each child—one box from a bar of soap, one sheet of color-coded dot stickers (such as Avery®).

Preparation: Cut dowels into 6-inch (15-cm) lengths—one for each child. Use knife to poke a hole slightly smaller than ¼ inch (.625 cm) in bottom of each soap box (sketch a). Cover work area with newspaper. Pour paint into shallow containers.

Instruct each child in the following procedures:

✦ Insert end of dowel into hole at bottom of box. Glue around hole to secure dowel in place (sketch b).

✦ Place several dried beans inside box through top flap. Close flap and seal with glue.

✦ Paint box and allow to dry.

✦ Use dot stickers to decorate box.

✦ Hold dowel and shake maracas to create your own rhythm.

Simplification Idea: Cover soap box with white paper and use felt pens to decorate.

Enrichment Ideas: Bring in actual maracas to show to children. Play a recording in which maracas are used and have children play along.

Family Talk:

Maracas are a popular rhythm instrument in Mexico. What is your favorite musical instrument? What instruments do your family members play? Some instruments take a lot of practice to learn how to play. And some are easy to play—like our maracas. Let's shake our maracas and make up our own song.

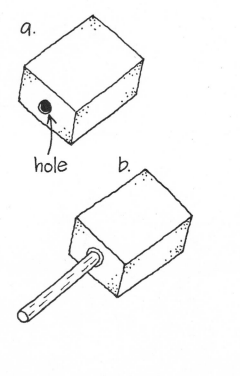

a.

hole

b.

Chinese Streamers

(10-15 MINUTES)

Materials: Crepe paper streamers in a variety of bright colors, string, foil star stickers, transparent tape, scissors, measuring stick. For each child—one large plastic or wooden thread spool.

Preparation: Remove labels from spools. Cut crepe paper into 1-yard (.9-m) lengths—three different colors for each child. Cut string into 18-inch (45-cm) lengths—one for each child.

Instruct each child in the following procedures:

✦ Fold one end of streamer into a point (sketch a). Repeat for other two streamers.

✦ Tape points of streamers onto spool (sketch b).

✦ Decorate streamers with star stickers.

✦ Thread string through center of spool. With teacher's help, tie a knot to secure string (sketch b).

✦ Hold spool by string and wave in the air. Wind streamers around spool when not in use.

Enrichment Idea: Instead of holding spool by string, make a long handle by inserting and gluing a dowel into center of spool (sketch c).

Family Talk:

Optional: Show China on a map. **In a country called China, children wave streamers like these during parades. Tell about a time when your family went to a parade. What did you see in the parade? What shapes can you make by waving your streamers in the air? Can you make a circle?**

Alley Cat

(15-20 MINUTES)

Materials: Yarn in a variety of colors, poster board, pencil, felt scraps, craft glue, scissors, measuring stick. For each child—two medium-size wiggle eyes, one small black pom-pom.

Preparations: Cut poster board into 3-inch (7.5-cm) squares—one for each child. Draw an *X* in the center of each square. Cut a slit on opposite sides of *X* as shown in sketch a. Cut yarn into 3-yard (.9-m) lengths—two for each child. Cut remaining yarn into 8-inch (20-cm) lengths—one for each child.

Instruct each child in the following procedures:

◆ Choose two colors of long yarn lengths. Wrap both pieces of yarn around poster board square, perpendicular to slits (sketch b).

◆ Slide smaller piece of yarn through slits. With teacher's help, pull ends together tightly and tie a knot (sketch c).

◆ Slide scissors through top edge of wrapped yarn and cut (sketch d). Repeat for bottom edge of wrapped yarn.

◆ Tear poster board away from yarn. Fluff yarn to make large pom-pom.

◆ Glue wiggle eyes onto pom-pom "alley cat." Glue black pom-pom for nose and felt scraps for ears and tongue.

Enrichment Idea: Make a family of cats or other animals using smaller (or larger) squares of poster board.

Family Talk:

What are you going to name your pet? Does your family have any pets? How can you help take good care of your pets? God made animals for us to take care of and enjoy. Let's thank God for the animals He created!

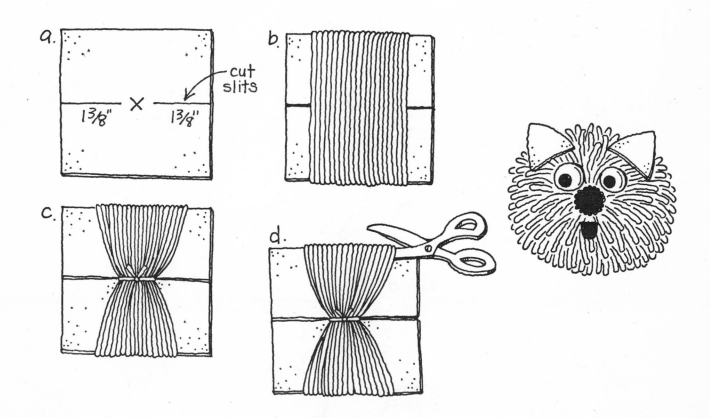

Zookeeper Magnets

(15-20 MINUTES)

Materials: Animal crackers, acrylic paint in a variety of colors, paintbrushes, shallow containers, clear nail polish, narrow magnet strips, craft glue, scissors, ruler, newspaper.

Preparation: Cut magnet strips into ½-inch (1.25-cm) lengths—two for each child. Cover work area with newspaper. Pour paint into shallow containers.

Instruct each child in the following procedures:

◆ Choose two unbroken crackers. (Note: Have extra crackers available as they break easily.)

◆ Paint front of crackers and allow to dry.

◆ In well-ventilated area, brush clear nail polish on fronts and backs of crackers. Let dry.

◆ Glue magnet piece onto back of each cracker (sketch a). Allow glue to dry.

Simplification Idea: Omit painting and just use clear nail polish. Or use clear acrylic spray instead of nail polish.

Enrichment Ideas: Make a jewelry pin by gluing a piece of poster board onto back of painted cracker. Glue pin back onto poster board (sketch b). Or glue painted cracker onto a barrette clip.

Family Talk:

What animals can we find in our animal cookies today? Have you ever been to the zoo? What is your favorite animal at the zoo? What is your (mom's) favorite animal at the zoo? Did you know that animals have families too? The zoo is a fun place to go with your family!

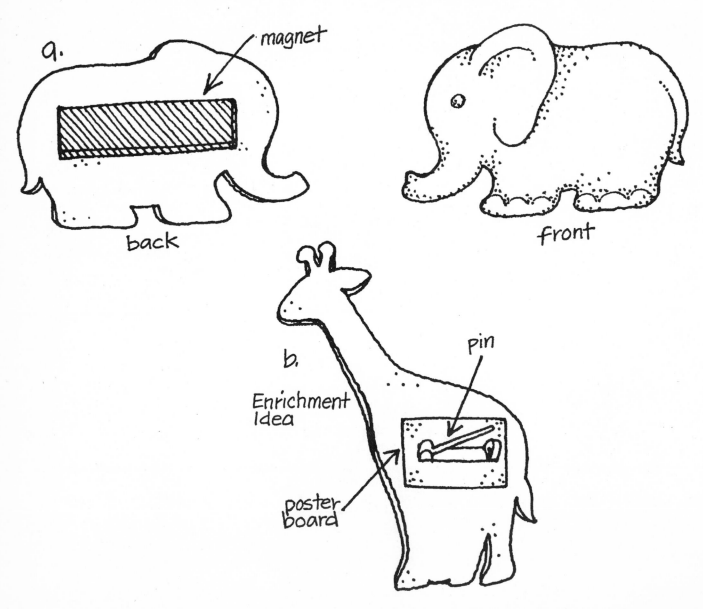

Section Two/Grades 1-3

Crafts for Younger Elementary

Children in the first few years of school delight in completing craft projects. They have a handle on most of the basic skills needed, they are eager to participate and their taste in art has usually not yet surpassed their ability to produce. In other words, they generally like the things they make.

Since reading ability is not a factor in most craft projects, crafts can be a great leveler among a group. Some children excel here who may or may not be top achievers in other areas.

Many of the projects in the section for young children also will appeal to younger elementary children.

Four-Window Photo Frame

(30-40 MINUTES)

Materials: Acrylic paint in a variety of colors, paintbrushes, shallow containers, jute, craft glue, craft knife, scissors, ruler, newspaper. For each child—15 tongue depressors.

Preparation: Use craft knife to score and break tongue depressors into 4-inch (10-cm) pieces—six for each child. Cut fabric scraps into 1x3-inch (2.5x7.5-cm) strips—eight for each child. Cut jute into 10-inch (25-cm) lengths—two for each child. Pour paint into shallow containers. Cover work area with newspaper.

Instruct each child in the following procedures:

✦ Place cut ends of tongue depressor pieces together to make three vertical rows as shown in sketch a.

✦ Glue a whole tongue depressor on top of each vertical piece (sketch b).

✦ Turn vertical pieces over. Place six whole tongue depressors horizontally across rows to make four windows (sketch c). Glue in place and allow to dry.

✦ Paint front of frame to look like an apartment building or house. Let dry.

✦ Glue one end of each jute piece onto top of frame. Tie loose ends of jute together in a bow.

✦ At home, glue four photographs onto back of frame. Hang picture frame on a hook or nail.

Simplification Idea: Decorate with felt pens instead of paint.

Enrichment Idea: Glue fabric scrap pieces onto sides of each window to make curtains (sketch d).

Family Talk:

What did you look like when you were a baby? Videos and photographs are some ways to see what you really looked like when you were younger. What did people do before the camera was invented? (Drew sketches or painted portraits of family members.) **What pictures will you put in your frame?**

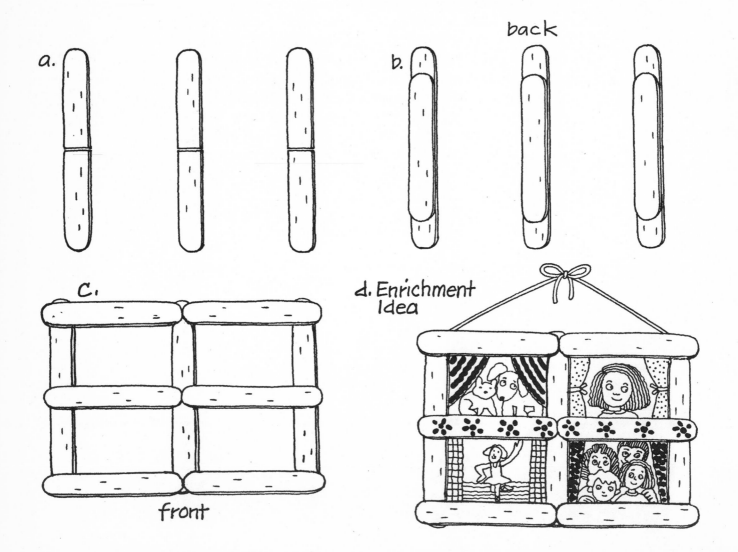

a.

b. back

c. front

d. Enrichment Idea

Family Jeans Scrapbook Cover

(20-30 MINUTES)

Materials: Sturdy wrapping paper in a variety of colors and patterns, discarded denim jeans, fabric paint, hole punches, transparent tape, glue, scissors. For each child—one large cereal box, one 38-inch (95-cm) shoelace.

Preparation: Cut top, bottom and one side out of each cereal box (sketch a). Cut entire back pockets out of blue jeans (sketch b)—one pocket for each child.

Instruct each child in the following procedures:

✦ Lay cereal box flat. Glue wrapping paper onto cereal box as you would a gift (sketch c).

✦ Crease box into original shape. Punch two holes in front and back covers (sketch d).

✦ Glue back of pocket onto front cover (sketch e).

✦ Use fabric paints to decorate or write name on pocket. Allow to dry.

✦ Tie shoelace through back and front holes (sketch e).

Enrichment Ideas: Glue buttons and plastic jewels onto pocket. Use fabric glue or hot glue to cover scrapbook with denim material instead of wrapping paper. Use white or orange fabric pen to draw stitch marks around border of scrapbook. Use scribble pads or brown paper bags cut into 12x19-inch (30x47.5-cm) sheets for scrapbook pages.

Family Talk:

Who in your family do you look most like? Who do you act most like? Our scrapbooks are made from blue jeans but there is another kind of genes. Genes are tiny particles in your body that determine your looks and personality. Your genes are a mixture of your mother's and father's genes. It's fun to look at yourself in the mirror and see what parts of you look like your mother and what parts look like your father!

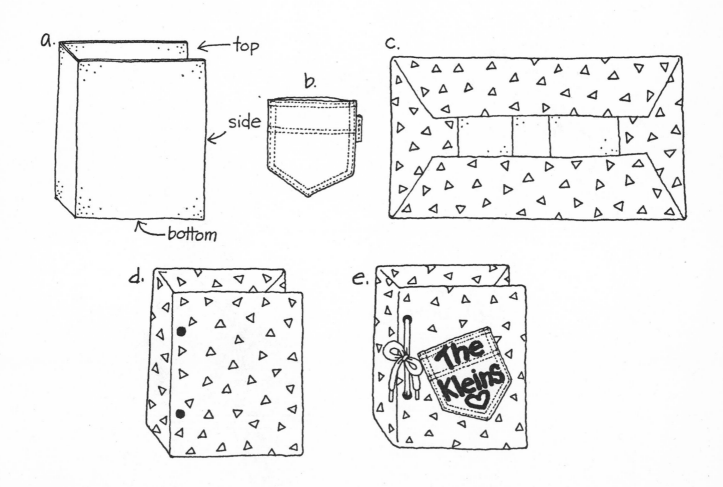

Easy Easel

Materials: Felt pens in a variety of colors, drill, ⅛-inch (.32-cm) drill bit, narrow ribbon, wood glue, measuring stick. For each child—three tongue depressors, two craft sticks.

Preparation: Cut ribbon into 14-inch (35-cm) lengths—one for each child. Drill hole at one end of each tongue depressor.

Instruct each child in the following procedures:

✦ Use felt pens to color and decorate tongue depressors and craft sticks.

✦ With teacher's help, glue craft sticks directly on top of each other.

✦ Thread ribbon through holes in tongue depressors. With teacher's help, secure ribbon with a knot or a bow (sketch a).

✦ Separate top two tongue depressors from the third one. Glue edge of craft sticks onto tongue depressors as shown in sketch a. Allow glue to dry.

✦ Arrange ends of tongue depressors in a triangular shape. Use easel to display postcards, greeting cards or photographs (sketch b).

Enrichment Ideas: Use acrylic paints instead of felt pens. Letter words of a memory verse on a large index card to display on easel.

Family Talk:

Artists use large easels to hold pictures and paintings. What do you like to paint pictures of? Who in your family is a good artist? What are you good at doing? Some people may be good artists and some may be good at sports, music or something else. We use the word "talent" to describe something a person is good at. God gave each person in your family a talent. Every person is special in his or her own way. Let's thank God for making each one of us special!

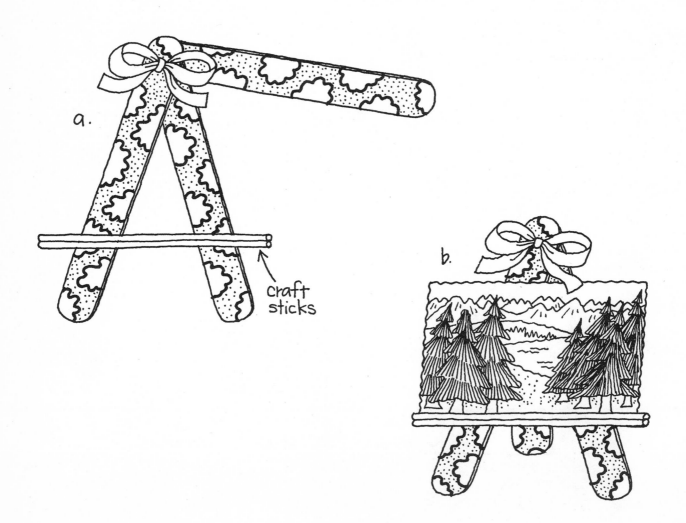

a.

craft sticks

b.

Family Message Board

Materials: Tempera paint in a variety of bright colors, paintbrushes, shallow containers, heavy white cardboard or foam-core board, wide magnetic strips, pencils, craft knife, glue, scissors, rulers, newspaper. For each child—three to five wooden clothespins (spring-type).

Preparation: Cut cardboard or foam-core board into 9x12-inch (22.5x30-cm) rectangles—one for each child. Cut magnetic strips into 5-inch (12.5-cm) lengths—two for each child. Cover work area with newspaper. Pour paint into shallow containers. Optional: Ask children to bring in small household items that would make good prints.

Instruct each child in the following procedures:

◆ Paint each clothespin a different color—one for each family member. Let dry.

◆ Glue magnet strip at top and bottom on back of message board.

◆ Dip ends of various items such as pencil erasers, rulers or forks into paint and press onto front of board to make prints (sketch a).

◆ Glue clothespins onto message board (sketch b).

◆ Place message board on refrigerator or other metal appliance at home. Clip drawings or notes of thanks, love, encouragement to a specific family member by attaching message to his or her colored clothespin.

Simplification Idea: Provide stickers instead of paint or ask children to bring in their favorite stickers to decorate message boards.

Enrichment Ideas: Cover cardboard with wrapping paper or self-adhesive paper. Glue sequins or jewels onto message board. With teacher's help, write names of family members on clothespins. Or draw shapes of plants and animals on poster board. Cut out shapes and glue onto front of clothespins (sketch c).

Family Talk:

What can you clip onto your message board? How do you feel when you get a kind card or picture from someone in your family? We can let our family members know we love them by writing a message, by drawing a picture, or by telling them!

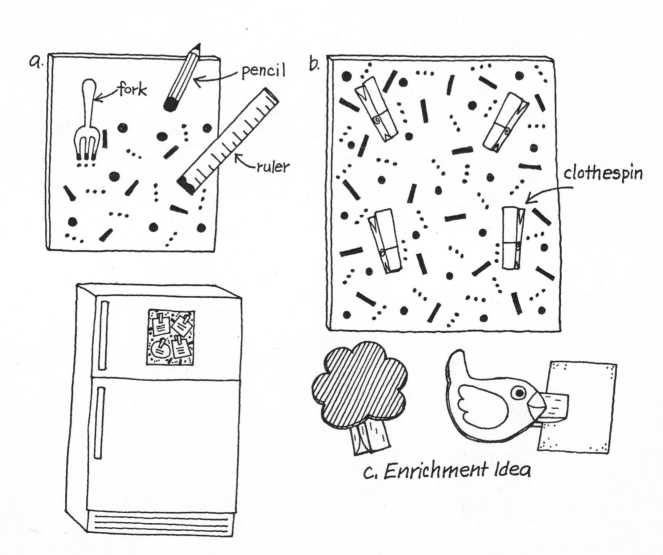

a.

fork

pencil

ruler

b.

clothespin

c. Enrichment Idea

Home-by-Night Banner

(20-30 MINUTES)

Materials: Black or navy felt, fabric scraps and ribbons in a variety of colors, white fabric, silver or gold sequins, ½-inch (1.25-cm) dowels or sticks, saw, sewing machine or needle and thread, yarn, permanent fine-tip felt pens, pencil, glue, scissors, ruler.

Preparation: Cut felt into 9x12-inch (22.5x30-cm) rectangles—one for each child. Fold over top of each felt rectangle about 1 inch (2.5 cm) and stitch to make a casing (sketch a). Cut ribbon into 5-inch (12.5-cm) lengths—three for each child. Saw dowels or sticks into 12-inch (30-cm) lengths—one for each child. Draw 3- to 4-inch (7.5- to 10-cm) stars onto white fabric and cut out—one for each child.

Instruct each child in the following procedures:

✦ Cut and glue fabric scraps onto felt banner to look like your home (sketch b).

✦ Use felt pen to letter a message on the star, such as "God bless our home."

✦ Choose three ribbons. Glue star at top corner of banner, attaching ends of ribbons underneath star.

✦ Glue sequins onto banner for additional stars.

✦ Slide dowel or stick through casing at top of banner.

✦ Cut yarn to desired hanging length. Tie one end of yarn to each side of dowel to make a hanger.

Simplification Idea: For younger children, cut fabric scraps into a variety of geometric shapes ahead of time.

Enrichment Idea: Children hand-stitch the casing.

Family Talk:

What does your home look like? Some people live in houses. Other people live in apartments, mobile homes or even boats! No matter what your home is like, it is a special place where you sleep, eat and spend time with your family. What else do you like to do at home? Let's ask God to bless us and keep us safe in our homes.

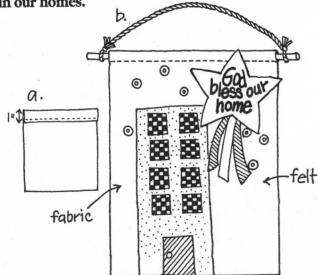

Sidewalk Chalk

**(TWO-DAY PROJECT/
15-20 MINUTES)**

Materials: Plaster of paris, powdered tempera paint in a variety of colors, large bowl of water, wax paper, vegetable oil, napkins, measuring cups, tablespoons, newspaper. For each child—one 10-oz. plastic cup, one toilet paper tube, one craft stick.

Preparation: Place ½ cup of plaster of paris in each plastic cup. Tear off a piece of wax paper for each child to work on. Cover work area with newspaper.

Instruct each child in the following procedures:

DAY ONE:

✦ Pour small amount of oil onto napkin and rub oil on the inside of cardboard tube.

✦ Choose paint color. Add ½ cup of powdered tempera paint to plaster in cup.

✦ Use craft stick to stir contents in cup.

✦ Add one tablespoon of water to mixture and stir until it looks like thick pudding. (If mixture is too dry, add a little more water.)

✦ Place end of cardboard tube on wax paper.

✦ Pour mixture into tube, almost to the top (sketch a). Allow at least 4 to 5 hours for chalk to dry.

DAY TWO:

✦ Tear tube away from chalk.

✦ Use chalk to draw on pavement. Erase with water.

Family Talk:

What message would you like to write on the sidewalk in front of your house or apartment? On a street where lots of cars go by? What message do you think God might want to write on a busy street? God has written a message to all people; it's the Bible!

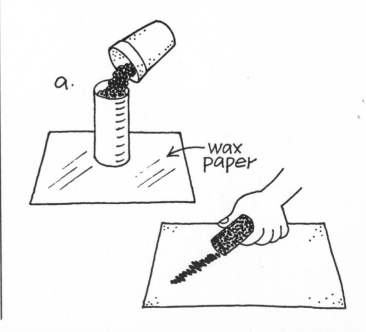

Celebration Tree

(25-30 MINUTES)

Materials: Plaster of paris, water, wire ornament hangers, variety of used greeting cards and/or wrapping paper, construction paper in a variety of colors, raffia, hammer, nail, piece of wood scrap, scissors, glue, pencils. For each child—one large can (such as a coffee can), a small tree branch with several limbs, one medium-size paper sack, three frozen-juice can lids (any size), paint stirring stick.

Preparation: Place juice can lids on scrap-wood surface. Use hammer and nail to make a hole at top of each lid (sketch a).

Instruct each child in the following procedures:

✦ Fill can two-thirds with plaster of paris and one-third with water. Use paint stirring stick to stir until creamy. (Note: Work rapidly, as mixture begins to harden very quickly.)

✦ Insert end of tree branch into center of can (sketch b). Hold in place until plaster begins to harden.

✦ Make ornaments for tree to celebrate your favorite holidays. Cut out pictures from greeting cards and wrapping paper, cut shapes from construction paper, or draw your own pictures to glue onto lids (sketch c).

✦ Insert end of wire hanger through hole in each juice can lid.

✦ When plaster is fairly dry, place can inside bag. Fold down top edge of bag (sketch d).

✦ Take several strands of raffia and tie around can to secure bag in place (sketch d).

✦ Make additional ornaments at home. Place ornaments on tree according to celebration. Or, glue photographs of family members onto juice can lids to create a "family tree."

Simplification Ideas: Use jars filled with gravel instead of plaster. Use chenille wire to make ornament hangers.

Enrichment Ideas: Cover can with wrapping paper or colorful self-adhesive paper. Paint tree branches using acrylic paint in a variety of bright colors. Make a chain of garland to decorate tree using interlocking strips of construction paper.

Family Facts:

What occasions does your family like to celebrate? How do you celebrate birthdays? How do you decorate for each celebration? Families are unique in the ways that they celebrate. Sometimes celebrations are based on traditions, passed on from generation to generation. And sometimes we make up our own ways to celebrate. You can decorate and redecorate your celebration tree to liven up any special occasion. Or use it for a "family tree!"

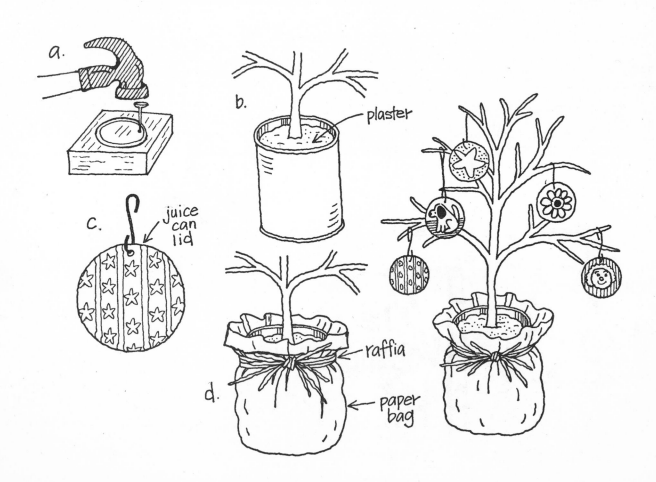

Vacation Keepsake Book

(25-30 MINUTES)

Materials: Tempera paint in a variety of colors, shallow containers, several cookie sheets, white or beige card stock, thin yarn, hole punches, plastic spoons, paper towels, transparent tape, scissors, measuring stick, newspaper. For each child—one marble, five resealable plastic sandwich bags.

Preparation: Cut the card stock into 7-inch (17.5-cm) squares—two for each child. Cut yarn into 18-inch (45-cm) lengths—one for each child. Wrap small piece of tape around one end of each yarn piece to make a needle. Pour thin layer of paint into shallow containers. Place a spoon in each color of paint. Line cookie sheets with newspaper. Cover work area with newspaper.

Instruct each child in the following procedures:

◆ Place card stock squares in cookie sheet.

◆ Dip marble in paint. Use spoon to remove marble and place marble on cookie sheet. Move cookie sheet around so that marble rolls over card stock to make a design (sketch a).

◆ Wipe paint off marble and repeat process with another color. Allow paint to dry.

◆ Lay sandwich bags directly on top of one another with openings facing same direction.

◆ Place one card stock square under sandwich bags and one on top, aligning all sides. Punch three evenly spaced holes on side opposite of bag openings (sketch b).

◆ Thread yarn up through bottom hole leaving about 4 inches (10 cm) of slack at bottom.

◆ Weave yarn through other holes as shown in sketch c.

◆ Thread yarn around spine of book and through holes as shown in sketch d.

◆ Tie loose ends of yarn together tightly at bottom of book (sketch e). Cut off excess yarn.

◆ Place postcards, leaves, photographs and other vacation memorabilia in resealable bags.

Simplification Idea: Punch holes in covers and bags ahead of time.

Enrichment Idea: Use felt pens to write title on front cover. Add more resealable bags.

Family Talk:

When you buy or collect things from a trip or special event they are called "souvenirs" or "keepsakes." What kinds of souvenirs have you saved? Souvenirs and keepsakes help us remember special places and events. When you're much older, you can look through your Vacation Keepsake Book to remind you of good times you had with your family and friends. Let's thank God for special memories!

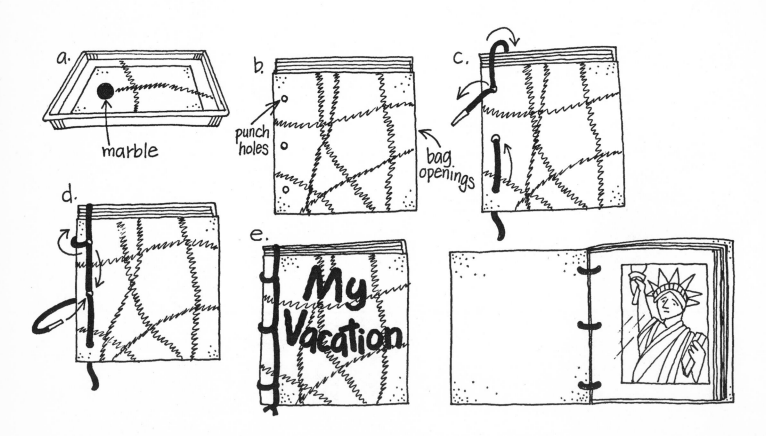

Celebration Comet

(10-15 MINUTES)

Materials: Fabric scraps; crepe paper streamers or Mylar strips; rags or old socks; string, yarn or bias tape; scissors; measuring stick.

Preparation: Cut fabric scraps into 7-inch (17.5-cm) squares—one for each child. Cut streamers or Mylar strips into 1-yard (.9-m) lengths—two for each child. Cut yarn or string into 8-inch (20-cm) lengths—one for each child.

Instruct each child in the following procedures:

✦ Place fabric square print side down. Lay middle of streamers or Mylar strips in the center of fabric square (sketch a).

✦ Place a small pile of rags or an old sock on top of strips (sketch a).

✦ Gather up edges of fabric and tie tightly with string, yarn or bias tape (sketch b).

✦ Throw comet up in the air and catch it. Or throw it to a friend across from you.

Enrichment Idea: Older children may measure and cut their own fabric, yarn and streamers.

Family Talk:

Have you ever looked up in the sky at night and seen a shooting star? A comet looks a lot like a shooting star, but it's larger. Today we're making a toy that looks like a comet. You can throw your comet in the air!

Japanese Kite

(30-40 MINUTES)

Materials: Permanent felt pens in a variety of colors, 3/16-inch (1/5-cm) dowels, saw, kite string, transparent or masking tape, scissors, measuring stick. For each child—one white plastic 13-gallon (49.4-L) garbage bag, one toilet paper tube or small wood scrap.

Preparation: Cut bottom seam off plastic bag. Draw kite outline on each plastic bag as shown in sketch a. Saw dowels into 29-inch (72.5-cm) lengths—two for each child. Cut string into 5-foot (15-m) lengths—one for each child. Cut additional string into 30-foot (9-m) lengths—one for each child.

Instruct each child in the following procedures:

◆ Cut along lines on plastic bag.

◆ Unfold kite. Use permanent felt pens to decorate kite.

◆ Turn kite over, decorated side down. Tape a dowel to each side of kite as shown in sketch b.

◆ Reinforce corners of kite with tape (sketch b).

◆ Use tip of scissors to poke a tiny hole in top two corners. Tie ends of shorter length of string through holes to make a bridle (sketch c).

◆ Tie a loop at midpoint of bridle. Tie end of longer length of string to loop. Wrap remaining string or "flying line" around toilet paper tube or wood scrap to make a kite reel.

◆ To fly kite: Take kite outside and hold it up. As wind begins to carry kite, slowly release string so kite rises with the wind.

Simplification Idea: For younger children, teacher cuts out kite ahead of time.

Enrichment Idea: Decorate kite reel.

Family Talk:

Kites are very popular in Japan. Optional: Show Japan on a map. **What makes kites fly? Wind! Can you see wind? We can't see God either, but we know He's there. You can talk to God at home, in the car, in your backyard—anywhere and He will be there. Sometimes your friends and family are too busy to listen—but God will always listen to your prayers!**

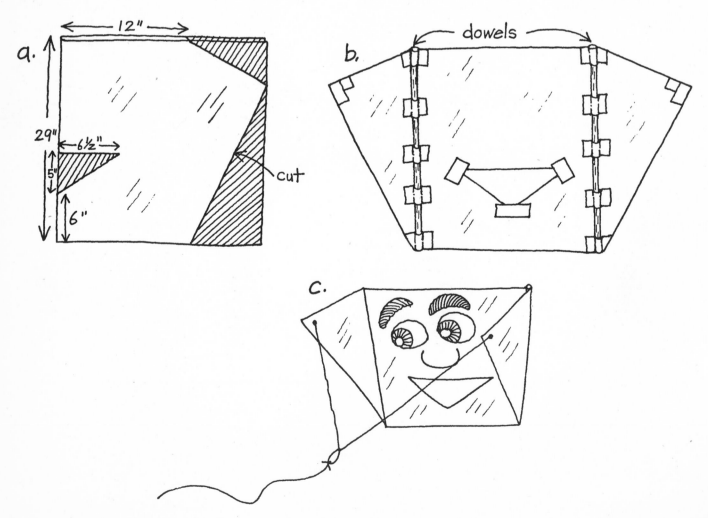

African Rattle

(TWO-DAY PROJECT/60 MINUTES)

Materials: Acrylic paint in a variety of bright colors, paint-brushes, shallow containers, dried beans, masking tape, permanent felt pens, water, glue, newspaper. For each child—one large round wooden clothespin (nonspring-type), one medium-size balloon, two paper towels.

Preparation: Mix two parts glue to one part water in containers. Cover work area with newspaper. Pour paint into shallow containers.

Instruct each child in the following procedures:

DAY ONE:

✦ Place several beans inside balloon.

✦ Blow the balloon up to a medium size. Tie a knot about 1-inch (2.5-cm) from lip of balloon.

✦ Insert end of clothespin into lip of balloon and secure with tape (sketch a).

✦ Wrap tape around clothespin to make a handle.

✦ Tear pieces of paper towel or newspaper into thin strips. Dip strips into glue mixture and use to cover balloon (sketch b).

✦ Let dry overnight.

DAY TWO:

✦ Paint rattle and allow to dry.

✦ Use permanent felt pens to draw a design on rattle.

✦ Shake rattle to create a rhythm.

Enrichment Idea: Use dried gourds instead of balloons and clothespins. Make a small opening in gourd and add beans. Cover hole with masking tape and paint with acrylic paint.

Family Talk:

Do you know anybody from Africa? Have any of your relatives ever been to Africa? In Africa, there are tribes of people who make rattles out of gourds. Optional: Show Africa on a map. **What is a gourd?** (A vegetable that looks like a cross between a squash and a pumpkin.) **Some Africans also use gourds to make bottles, bowls, dishes and toys. Let's use our rattles to praise God here and at home!**

a. tape

b.

31

Communication Can

(15-20 MINUTES)

Materials: White construction paper, writing paper, typewriter, photocopier, fine-tip felt pens, transparent tape, scissors, glue. For each child—one cylinder canister (such as an oatmeal or bread crumb container), six small glittery pompoms, one sheet of color-coded dot stickers (such as Avery®).

Preparation: Cut construction paper into rectangles large enough to wrap around container—one for each child. Type suggested conversation starters on writing paper and photocopy—one for each child. Cut conversation starters into small strips and place in canisters.

Instruct each child in the following procedures:

✦ Use felt pens to draw various faces on the dot stickers—happy, sad, afraid, surprised, angry (sketch a).

✦ Letter "Communication Can" in center of construction paper.

✦ Stick dots randomly onto construction paper.

✦ Wrap construction paper around container and tape in place.

✦ Glue pom-poms onto canister for decoration.

✦ Place conversation strips in Communication Can.

✦ At mealtime, pass the Communication Can around the table. Each family member draws a conversation strip and answers the question on his or her strip.

CONVERSATION STRIPS:

✦ Tell about something funny that happened to you today.

✦ What did you see that God created today?

✦ How were you a helper today?

✦ What kind words did someone say today?

✦ What was the best part of your day?

✦ Tell about something that you did in the morning.

✦ Tell about something you did in the afternoon.

✦ What did you learn today?

✦ How did God take care of you today?

✦ What can you thank God for today?

Enrichment Idea: Older children can make up their own conversation starters and cut out their own conversation strips.

Family Talk:

When is a good time for your whole family to get together each day and talk? Some families talk at mealtime! God planned for our families to listen and talk to each other. Using your Communication Can will be a fun way to start conversations.

a.

Bubble Art Stationery

(10-15 MINUTES)

Materials: Powdered tempera paint in a variety of colors, 8½x11-inch (21.5x27.5-cm) white paper, water, dish soap, newspaper. For each child—a drinking straw, one pie tin.

Preparation: Cut paper in half—several sheets for each child. Pour a small amount of dish soap and water into each pie tin. Cover work area with newspaper.

Instruct each child in the following procedures:

✦ Choose paint color. Use end of straw to mix a small amount of powdered tempera paint into water mixture.

✦ Place end of straw into paint mixture and blow into straw until bubbles appear on surface (sketch a). (Note: Have younger children practice blowing into straw—not sucking.)

✦ Gently lay paper on top of bubbles only. Bubbles will stick to paper, then collapse, leaving a colorful print. Allow paper to dry.

✦ Trade pie tins with other children to make additional colors on stationery. Wash end of straw before using other colors.

✦ Use stationery at home to write simple notes to friends and relatives.

Family Talk:

When have you received a letter or card in the mail? It's fun to get mail. We can write notes on our stationery to send to friends and relatives who live far away. Who will you send a letter to?

a.

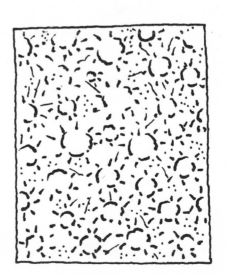

Jump Rope

(15-20 MINUTES)

Materials: Acrylic paints, clear acrylic spray paint, paintbrushes, shallow containers, rope, ¾-inch (1.9-cm) dowels, saw, ¾-inch (.32-cm) and ⅛-inch (.94-cm) drill bits, drill, sandpaper, masking tape, scissors, measuring stick, newspaper.

Preparation: Saw dowels into 5-inch (12.5-cm) pieces—two for each child. Use small drill bit to drill a small pilot hole about ¾-inch (1.9 cm) from end of each dowel piece (sketch a). Use large bit to drill final hole in each dowel piece (sketch b). Cut rope or cording into 3-yard (.9-m) lengths—one for each child. Cover work area with newspaper. Pour paint into shallow containers.

Instruct each child in the following procedures:

◆ Use sandpaper to smooth any rough edges on dowel pieces.

◆ Paint dowel pieces.

◆ In well-ventilated area, spray dowel pieces with clear spray and allow to dry (about two minutes).

◆ Wrap a piece of tape around ends of rope to prevent fraying.

◆ Thread rope through holes in dowels and tie knots to secure (sketch c).

◆ Your rope is ready for hopping, skipping and jumping!

Family Talk:

Jump Rope is a popular game played by kids all over the world. How many times can you jump rope without missing? If you are good at jumping you might want to try the following: "Double Hopping" (add a second jump while the rope is over head); "Left, Right" (jump on one foot and then the other); "Rocking" (place one foot ahead of the other, jumping first on the front foot and then on the back foot). Show your friends and family the different ways you can jump rope!

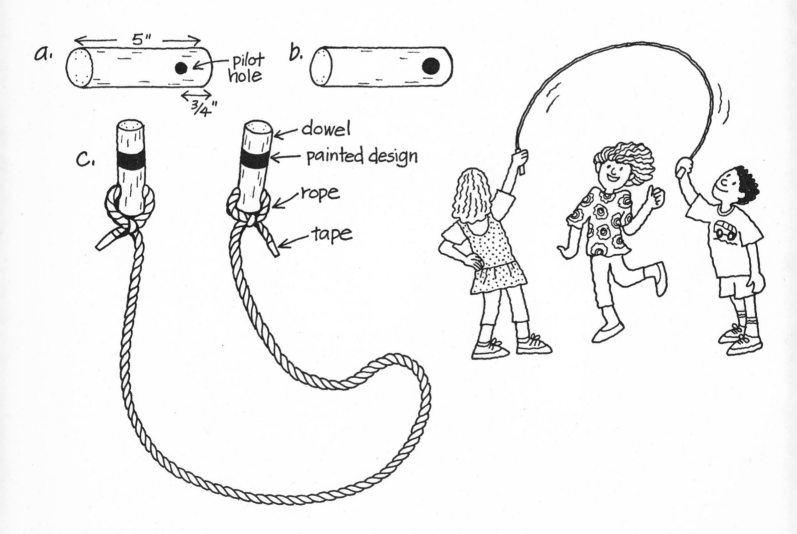

City Street

(30-60 MINUTES)

Materials: Tempera paint in a variety of colors, paintbrushes, shallow containers, several kinds of discarded food containers (such as cereal or cracker boxes and milk cartons), cardboard, butcher paper, pencils, black felt pens, transparent tape, glue, craft knife, scissors, measuring stick, newspaper.

Preparation: Rinse out food containers and allow to dry. Cut cardboard into 1x2-foot (.3x.6-m) rectangles—one for each child. Cover work area with newspaper. Pour paint into shallow containers.

Instruct each child in the following procedures:

✦ Choose several food containers to use for buildings.

✦ Wrap each container in butcher paper or newspaper and secure with tape, as you would a gift (sketch a).

✦ Paint each covered container to look like a house, store or other building.

✦ Use felt pens to add familiar details so that buildings resemble structures in your town. Let dry.

✦ Glue buildings onto cardboard base (sketch b).

✦ Paint a street and sidewalk on cardboard base.

Simplification Idea: Use felt pens instead of paints to decorate buildings and street.

Enrichment Ideas: Use toilet paper tubes and construction paper to make trees, stop signs, traffic signals, vehicles and people figures to add to your city street. Children work in groups to make several streets, then place streets together to form a town.

Family Talk:

What is on the street where you live? What do you like about your street? What do you dislike? Does everyone on your street get along? What might help people on your street be better friends? The Bible says to "love your neighbor as yourself" (Matthew 22:39). Who are your neighbors?

Home "Sweet" Home

(20-30 MINUTES)

Materials: Graham crackers, powdered sugar, lemon juice, eggs, salt, medium-size bowl, measuring cups and spoons, electric mixer, plastic sandwich bags, colorful candies such as Skittles® or M&Ms®, sturdy cardboard, aluminum foil, glue, scissors or craft knife, ruler.

Preparation: Cut cardboard into 2½-inch (6.25-cm) squares and 12-inch (30-cm) squares—one of each for each child. Cover larger square with aluminum foil to make a platform for the house. The following recipe will make enough icing for eight children: Beat 3 cups powdered sugar, 2 egg whites, ¼ teaspoon salt and 2 teaspoons lemon juice for five minutes or until fluffy. Pour equal amounts of icing into eight sandwich bags. Squeeze icing into corner of bag and tie top of bag in a knot (sketch a).

Instruct each child in the following procedures:

◆ Glue small cardboard square onto foil-covered platform.

◆ Cut a small piece off the corner of bag of icing.

◆ Squeeze a generous line of icing around edges of small cardboard square (sketch b).

◆ Stand up half a graham cracker in icing to form front of house (sketch c).

◆ Add sides and back to house in same manner, squeezing icing in between crackers (sketch d).

◆ Use icing to attach two crackers on top of house to form roof.

◆ Use icing and candy pieces to customize house with a door, windows, shingles, a walkway leading to the house, etc.

Simplification Ideas: For younger children, build houses ahead of time and allow children to decorate. Or cut off top half of milk carton (half-gallon size) and use icing to glue graham crackers onto edges of carton.

Enrichment Ideas: Cut two triangles from brightly colored paper to fill in front and back roof spaces. Provide a variety of healthy food items such as raisins, nuts and cereal to decorate houses.

Family Talk:

What would your dream house be like? What do you like about the home you live in now? What have you and your family done to make the place where you live better? How do you help take care of your home? Let's thank God for giving us a place to call home!

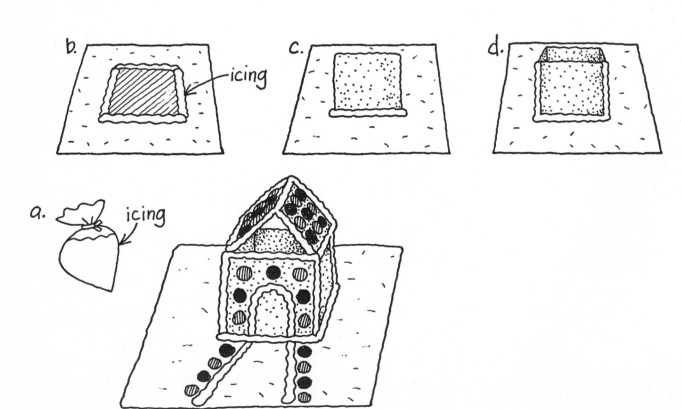

Wind Clanger

(20-30 MINUTES)

Materials: Tempera paint in a variety of colors, paintbrushes, shallow containers, clear acrylic spray, hammer, nail, heavy string, scissors, measuring stick, newspaper. For each child—one medium-size jingle bell, two tin cans (one with a larger circumference than the other, height may vary).

Preparation: Use hammer and nail to make a hole in the center of each tin can bottom. Cut string into 2-foot (.6-m) lengths—one for each child. Cover work area with newspaper. Pour paint into shallow containers.

Instruct each child in the following procedures:

◆ Paint a colorful design on bottoms and sides of cans (sketch a). Let dry.

◆ In well-ventilated area, spray cans with clear spray and allow to dry.

◆ Thread string through hole in can with smaller circumference (sketch b).

◆ Tie jingle bell to end of string. Tie a large knot several inches from bell to secure bell inside of can (sketch b).

◆ Tie another large knot in string outside top of can (sketch c).

◆ Thread loose end of string through other can.

◆ Make a large loop at end of string to hang Wind Clanger (sketch d).

◆ Hang Wind Clanger in a tree. Listen to the sounds it makes when the wind blows.

Simplification Ideas: Omit jingle bell and use clanging of cans for noisemaker. Or, omit smaller can and use only the jingle bell for a noisemaker.

Family Talk:

Our neighborhoods are filled with many noises. What noises do you hear on your street? What noises come from your house? Which noises are happy sounds? Unhappy? What do you think about when everything is very quiet and still? The Bible says, "Be still, and know that I am God" (Psalm 46:10).

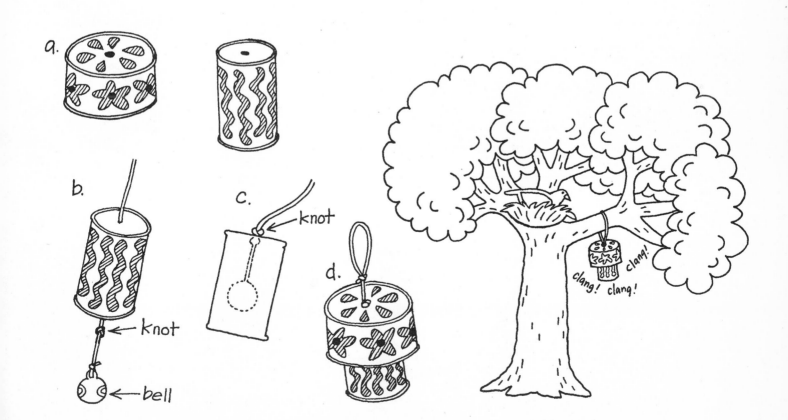

Boogie Bugs

(20-30 MINUTES)

Materials: Bug Pattern, toilet paper tubes, poster board, construction paper, felt pens, pencils, craft glue, scissors, ruler. For each child—one small marble, two small wiggle eyes.

Preparations: Cut poster board into 1x2-inch (2.5x5-cm) rectangles—two for each child. Trace Bug Pattern onto remaining poster board and cut out several patterns. Cut tubes into 3/4-inch (1.9-cm) hoops—one for each child. Cut construction paper into ¼x2-inch (.625x5-cm) strips—four for each child.

Instruct each child in the following procedures:

✦ Bend hoops into oval shapes.

✦ Trace Bug Pattern onto each poster board rectangle and cut out to make two side pieces.

✦ Glue one side piece onto edge of hoop (sketch a). Let dry.

✦ Place marble inside hoop.

✦ Glue second side piece onto other edge of hoop. Let dry.

✦ Glue wiggle eyes on front of bug (sketch b). Use felt pens to draw a face.

✦ Glue three construction paper strips underneath bug for legs. Fold additional strip into a *V* and glue above eyes for antennae.

✦ Place bug on a gentle slope and watch it boogie!

Enrichment Idea: Children can use felt pens to give their bugs stripes or spots.

Family Talk:

What kinds of bugs have you found around your home? Did you know that in some countries people keep bugs for pets? In Japan many people have pet crickets and fireflies. What pets do you have at home? God gave us animals to enjoy. He wants us to take good care of our pets and treat them nicely.

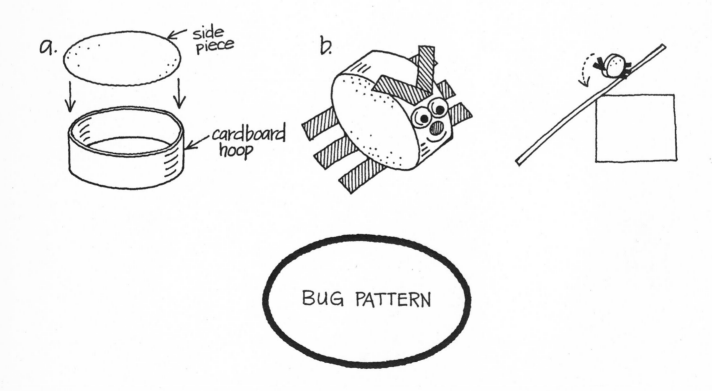

a. side piece

cardboard hoop

b.

BUG PATTERN

Ring-the-Stick Game

(20-30 MINUTES)

Materials: Toilet paper or paper towel tubes, tempera paint, paintbrushes, shallow containers, cotton string, self-adhesive paper in colorful patterns, hole punch, masking tape, scissors, measuring stick, newspaper. For each child—one unsharpened pencil.

Preparation: Cut cardboard tubes into 1-inch (2.5-cm) lengths—two for each child. Cut string into 30-inch (75-cm) lengths—one for each child. Cut self-adhesive paper into ½x20-inch (1.25x50-cm) strips—one for each child. Cover work area with newspaper. Pour paint into shallow containers.

Instruct each child in the following procedures:

✦ Cut open two cardboard tube pieces (sketch a).

✦ Use masking tape to join the two pieces together to make a larger ring (sketch b).

✦ Punch a hole in ring.

✦ Paint the outside of ring and allow to dry.

✦ Peel backing from self-adhesive paper strip. Hold one end of string on pencil while spiraling paper strip tightly around length of pencil (sketch c).

✦ Tie loose end of string through hole in ring.

✦ Hold pencil with one hand and toss ring in the air, trying to catch it on the stick.

Simplification Idea: Use a wooden ring (available at most craft stores) instead of making one from cardboard tube.

Enrichment Ideas: Spray cardboard ring with acrylic spray paint. Or, cover ring with self-adhesive paper or wrapping paper.

Family Talk:

Ring-the-Stick is a game played by children who live in the country of India. Optional: Show India on a map. **Do you know anybody from India? People play games all over the world. Some games you can play by yourself, some you can play with a partner and some games you can play with many people. What games do you play with your family? At school?**

a. cut open

b.

c. string backing self-adhesive tape

Three-Key Holder

Materials: Acrylic paint in a variety of colors, clear acrylic spray, paintbrushes, shallow containers, permanent fine-tip felt pens, drill, 1/16-inch (.16-cm) drill bit, sandpaper, craft glue, scissors, ruler, newspaper. For each child—one precut wooden shape (available at craft stores), three 3/4-inch (1.9-cm) cup hooks.

Preparation: Drill three holes in each wood shape at least 1½ inches (3.75 cm) apart (see sketch). Cut ribbon into 10-inch (25-cm) lengths—two for each child. Cover work area with newspaper. Pour paint into shallow containers.

Instruct each child in the following procedures:

◆ Use sandpaper to smooth rough edges on wood.
◆ Paint wooden shape and allow to dry.
◆ Use felt pen to letter "Family Keys" at top of wooden shape.
◆ In well-ventilated area, spray key holder with clear spray and allow to dry.
◆ Glue ribbon onto each side of wood shape as shown in sketch.
◆ Screw cup hooks into drilled holes.

Enrichment Idea: Use fine-tip permanent felt pens to letter the three keys to good communication (listed below) next to cup hooks.

Family Talk:

What are the keys in your house used for? What happens when someone in your family loses their keys? We use keys to lock and unlock valuable items. We also use the word "key" to mean an "important point." For example, there are three keys to good communication. Do you know what they are? (Listen, be kind, tell the truth.) **Let's ask God to help us remember these very important keys for communicating with our families.**

ribbon

Address Plate

(15-20 MINUTES)

Materials: Acrylic paint in a variety of bold colors, clear acrylic spray paint, small paintbrushes, shallow containers, pencils, newspaper. For each child—one 8-inch (20-cm) square clay tile (available at building supply stores), one plate hanger.

Preparation: Cover work area with newspaper. Pour paint into shallow containers.

Instruct each child in the following procedures:

✦ Use pencil to sketch address number on tile. Make numbers large enough to cover most of tile space.

✦ Sketch a simple border around edge of tile.

✦ Attach plate hanger to tile using manufacturer's instructions. (Note: If tile is too heavy for plate hanger, drill a small hole in back of tile and hang on a nail.)

✦ Paint numbers and border. (Bold colors will show up best.) Let dry.

✦ In well-ventilated area, spray tile with clear spray and allow to dry.

✦ Ask parent's permission to hang tile on the front of house or apartment.

Simplification Idea: Use crayons instead of acrylic paint.

Family Talk:

Knowing a person's address can help you find his or her house or apartment even if you've never been there before. What is your address? I'm glad that God knows where each of us lives. He doesn't need to look up our addresses to find us. He is with us all the time.

paint

283

clay tile

283

Mexican Yarn Art

(25-30 MINUTES)

Materials: Rug yarn in a variety of colors, cardboard, self-adhesive paper, glue, scissors, measuring stick.

Preparation: Cut the cardboard into 9-inch (22.5-cm) squares—one for each child. Cut adhesive paper into 9-inch (22.5-cm) squares—one for each child. Glue nonsticky side of adhesive paper directly on top of cardboard square (sketch a). Cut yarn into 2-foot (.6-m) lengths—three different colors for each child.

Instruct each child in the following procedures:

◆ Remove backing from adhesive paper. Arrange one length of yarn into outline of a large enclosed shape. Press yarn onto adhesive paper so it sticks. Cut off excess yarn (sketch b).

◆ Choose a different color of yarn and lay it directly next to previous piece of yarn (sketch c). Continue to fill in shape with yarn, working from the outside in. Cut yarn as needed. Fill all blank spaces with yarn.

◆ With teacher's help, cut cardboard around the shape (sketch d).

◆ Use Yarn Art at home as a coaster, mat or hang as a picture.

Simplification Idea: Stick yarn onto adhesive paper in simple spiral design, starting in the center and working out.

Enrichment Idea: For older children, use glue instead of adhesive paper.

Family Talk:

What did we use to make our designs today? Yarn! What else can we use yarn for? We use yarn to make blankets, sweaters and other kinds of clothes. Where did you get the clothes you are wearing today? God gave each of you someone to take care of you by providing food, clothing and a place to live. Let's thank God for parents and other people who take care of us!

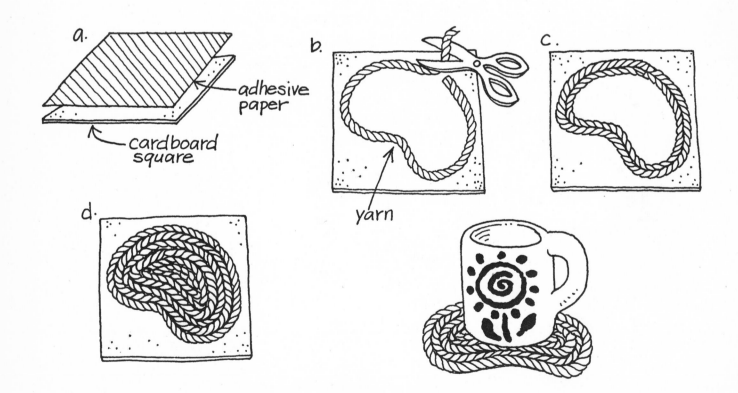

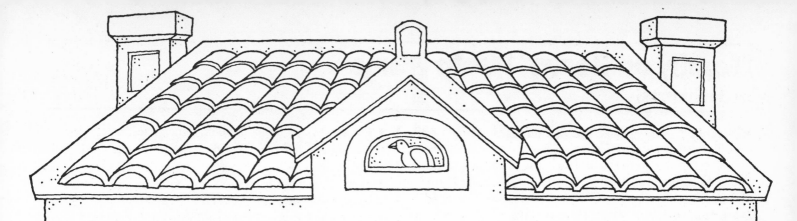

Section Three/Grades 4-6
Crafts for Older Elementary

Trying to plan craft projects for older children has driven many teachers prematurely gray. The challenge is that while these children have well-developed skills to complete projects, they also have well-developed preferences about what they want to do. Thus a project that may challenge their abilities may be scorned because it somehow is not appealing to these young sophisticates. Then the next project will seem too juvenile to the adult, but will click with the kids!

There's no justice! And a sense of humor surely helps. One helpful device is to filter a craft idea through a panel of experts—two or three fifth graders. If they like it, chances are the rest of the group will, also. Then, the better you get to know your particular students, the better your batting average will be.

We think you'll find projects in this section to satisfy the varied tastes of older elementary children!

"Family on Board" Photo Frame

(20-30 MINUTES)

Materials: Yellow poster board, cardboard, ⅛-inch (.32-cm) black graphic tape (such as Formaline®, available at graphics supply stores), nail, black felt pens, pencils, craft knife, glue, scissors, rulers. For each child—one 1¾-inch (4.4-cm) suction cup with hook (available at craft stores).

Preparation: Cut poster board into 8-inch (20-cm) squares—one for each child. Cut a 3x4½-inch (7.5x11.25-cm) opening from the center of each poster board square as shown in sketch a. Cut cardboard into 8-inch (20-cm) squares—one for each child. Use craft knife to score one side and cut three sides of a 3½x5-inch (8.75x12.5-cm) opening from each cardboard square as shown in sketch b.

Instruct each child in the following procedures:

- Glue poster board square onto cardboard square so that openings match up (sketch c).
- Use pencil to sketch a ½-inch (1.25-cm) border around the edge of poster board square (sketch c).

- Cut and place graphic tape on pencil lines.
- Use a thick felt pen to letter "(Smith) Family on Board" on frame.
- Use nail to poke a hole at top corner of frame (sketch d). Insert hook of suction cup through hole.
- Take frame home. Open cardboard flap opening. Place photograph onto front of flap and close (sketch e). Press suction cup on window or mirror to hang picture frame.

Family Talk:

What road signs have you seen that are the shape of your photo frame? What is the longest drive you and your family have taken? What games does your family play in the car? Road trips can be a great way to spend time talking and playing with your family.

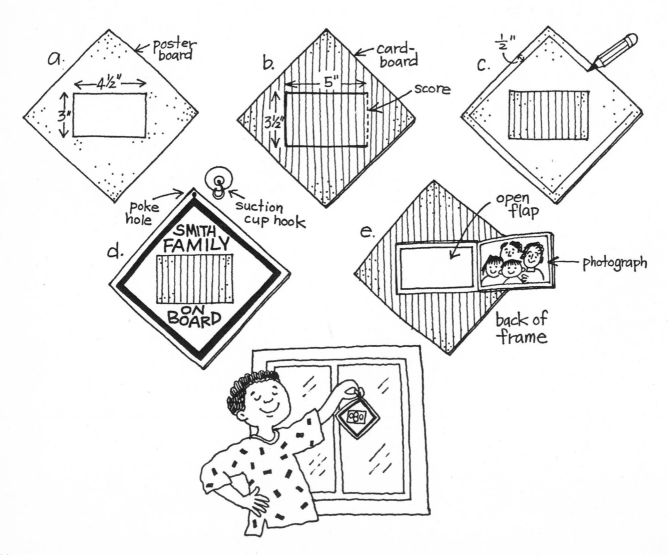

Corkboard Family Scrapbook

(30-45 MINUTES)

Materials: Thin adhesive-backed corkboard, cardboard, felt, drill, ¼-inch (.625-cm) drill bit, pencil, glue, scissors, measuring stick. For each child—three metal binder rings.

Preparation: Cut cardboard into 9x12-inch (22.5x30-cm) rectangles—two for each child. Cut cork into 12x19-inch (30x47.5-cm) rectangles—one for each child. Cut felt into 12x19-inch (30x47.5) rectangles—one for each child. Save felt scraps.

Instruct each child in the following procedures:

✦ Peel adhesive backing from cork piece. Line up edges of cardboard pieces onto cork piece, leaving a 1-inch (2.5-cm) gap in the center (sketch a).

✦ Glue large felt piece onto cardboard pieces, on side opposite of cork.

✦ Fold book in half and mark three evenly spaced holes as shown in sketch b. With teacher's help, drill holes through cardboard, felt and cork.

✦ Attach metal rings through holes.

✦ Cut felt shapes into letters and shapes. Glue onto corkboard to decorate scrapbook (sketch c).

Simplification Ideas: Cover both sides of cardboard with felt instead of using cork. Or, cover cardboard with self-adhesive paper.

Enrichment Idea: Use scribble pads or brown paper bags cut into 12x19-inch (30x47.5-cm) sheets for scrapbook pages.

Family Talk:

Why do people make and keep scrapbooks? Scrapbooks are a good place to keep pictures, cards, awards and other special reminders of the good times we've had with our families and friends. What is a special time with your family you'll never forget?

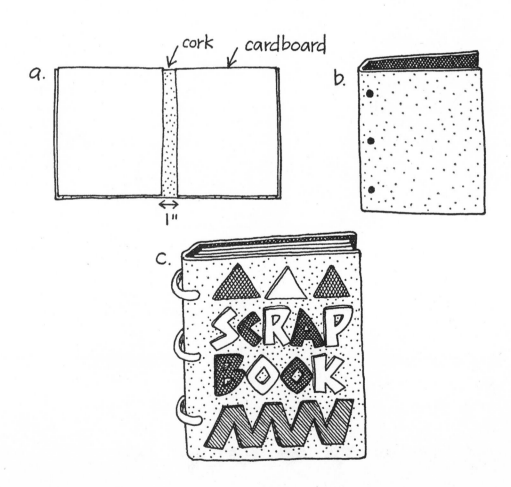

a. cork cardboard 1"

b.

c. SCRAP BOOK

Stamps with Sole

(15-20 MINUTES)

Materials: Several clean large shoe insoles, rubber cement, colored ink pads, disposable wet tissues, writing paper, ballpoint pens, scissors. For each child—two medium-size jar lids or small wood blocks.

Preparation: Cut insoles into three even pieces—one piece for each child.

Instruct each child in the following procedures:

✦ Draw a simple shape, such as a heart, star, initial, flower, onto smooth latex side of each insole piece. (Note: Letters and shapes are reversed when stamped—draw initials backwards.)

✦ Cut out shapes (sketch a).

✦ Glue cutouts onto jar lids or wood blocks to make rubber stamps (sketch b). Allow glue to dry.

✦ Press rubber stamp onto ink pad and then onto paper.

✦ Wipe stamps clean using disposable wet tissues.

Enrichment Ideas: Children work in groups and share rubber stamps and ink pads to decorate stationery, greeting cards and envelopes.

Family Talk:

What are your initials? Some people's first, middle and last initial, when put together, form a new word. Initials are a quick way to identify your name. Do you know why your parents gave you your name? What does your name mean? Many names used today can be found in the Bible. What are some you can think of?

a.

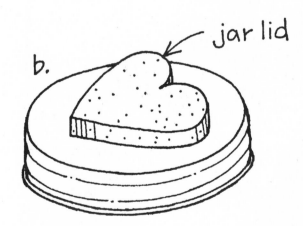

b.   jar lid

Sand-Painted Stationery

(15-20 MINUTES)

Materials: Very fine sandpaper, 8½x11-inch (21.5x27.5-cm) white paper, crayons, iron(s), ironing board, scissors, ruler, newspaper.

Preparation: Cut sandpaper into 2x5-inch (5x12.5-cm) rectangles—one for each child. Cut white paper in half—several sheets for each child. Cover ironing board with newspaper.

Instruct each child in the following procedures:

✦ Use crayons to draw a design on sandpaper (sketch a). Color heavily.

✦ Lay white paper on ironing board. Place colored sandpaper facedown on top edge of paper (sketch b). With teacher's help, iron until design is transferred to paper.

✦ Make additional sheets of stationery by applying more color to original design and ironing onto another sheet of paper.

✦ Use stationery at home to write letters.

Enrichment Idea: Children create complementary designs to decorate back flap of envelopes.

Family Talk:

Native Americans are known for the beautiful sand paintings they create. Do you know any Native American Indians? Who will you write to on your sand-painted stationery? How do you feel when you get a letter in the mail? How do you think (your grandmother) will feel when she gets your letter?

"This-Is-Me" Mask

(20-30 MINUTES)

Materials: Panty hose in a variety of shades; fabric, felt and paper scraps; brown, black, orange and yellow yarn; buttons; ribbon; sequins; pliers; several mirrors; glue; scissors. For each child—one wire coat hanger.

Preparation: Cut legs off of panty hose—one stocking for each child. Use pliers to bend each coat hanger into an oval shape (sketch a).

Instruct each child in the following procedures:

◆ Look in mirror and notice the shape of your face. With teacher's help, bend coat hanger to resemble shape of your face.

◆ Choose a stocking that resembles your skin color. Pull foot of stocking over wire shape. Tie end of stocking in a knot near hook and cut off excess (sketch b).

◆ Look in mirror and notice the color and shape of your eyes, mouth, nose and hair. Cut and glue materials onto stocking to make a mask that looks like you (sketch c).

Enrichment Idea: Children write several positive sentences describing themselves. They hold masks in front of their faces as they say their descriptions aloud.

Family Talk:

There is no one exactly like you! You are a unique combination of size, shape, color, personality, strengths and weaknesses! On a chalkboard, draw different shapes as you say, **Some people's faces are oval-shaped. Others are round or more like a triangle. What shape is your face? What color are your eyes? Your hair? What shape is your nose? God loves you and created you just the way you are!**

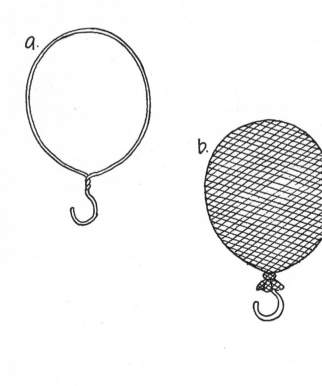

Friends-Around-the-World Mobile

(TWO-DAY PROJECT/50-60 MINUTES)

Materials: Acrylic paint in a variety of colors including yellow, red, brown, black and beige; small paintbrushes; shallow containers; fishing line; craft glue; scissors; ruler; newspaper. For each child—four large flat wooden clothespins (nonspring-type), four ¾-inch (1.9-cm) wooden balls, five chenille wires in a variety of colors.

Preparation: Cut some of the chenille wires into 6-inch (15-cm) lengths—four for each child. Cut fishing line into 10-inch (25-cm) lengths—five for each child. Cover work area with newspaper. Pour paint into shallow containers.

Instruct each child in the following procedures:

DAY ONE:

✦ Paint each clothespin a different color. Let dry.

✦ Paint each wooden ball a different flesh-tone color. Let dry.

✦ Glue painted ball onto top of each painted clothespin to form a head (sketch a). Allow glue to dry.

DAY TWO:

✦ Twist piece of chenille wire around top notch of each clothespin to make arms (sketch a). Pull ends tightly.

✦ Form a circle with an uncut piece of chenille wire. Twist ends together to secure.

✦ Twist the "arms" of each clothespin around the circle (sketch b).

✦ Tie ends of four lengths of fishing line onto circle at places where arms intersect (sketch c).

✦ Gather loose ends of fishing line and tie together. Make a loop with additional fishing line and tie at intersecting points of other fishing lines.

✦ Hang from window or ceiling.

Simplification Idea: Use round-headed clothespins and paint top of clothespin for head.

Enrichment Idea: Glue fabric scraps on clothespins to make clothes.

Family Talk:

What does this mobile represent to you? Why did God create people to be different? What would the world be like if everyone looked the same? When God looks at us, He looks beyond the color of our skin or the clothes we wear. He sees us and loves us for who we are on the inside!

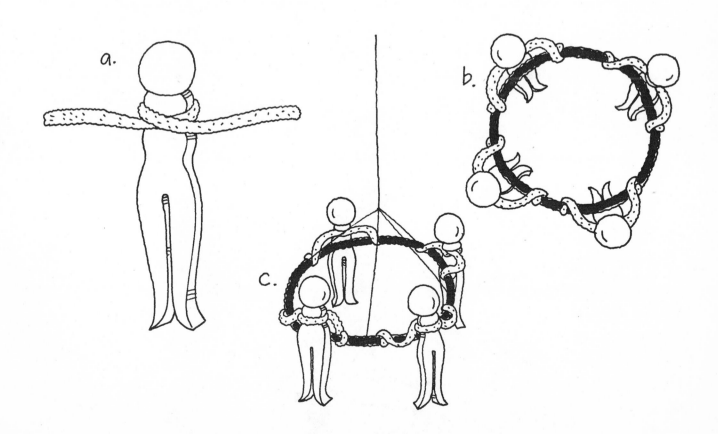

Homemade Kite

(25-30 MINUTES)

Materials: Sturdy wrapping paper in bold prints, kite string, 3/16-inch (1/5-cm) dowels, saw, white plastic trash bags, transparent or masking tape, pencils, rulers, scissors, measuring stick. For each child—one toilet paper tube or wood scrap. (Safety Note: Never use metal such as wire, tinsel or foil to make a kite.)

Preparation: Saw dowels into 18-inch (45-cm) lengths and 24-inch (60-cm) lengths—one of each length for each child. Cut wrapping paper into 18x24-inch (45x60-cm) rectangles—one for each child. Cut string into 30-foot (9-m) lengths—one for each child. Cut trash bags into 1x14-inch (2.5x35-cm) strips—three for each child.

Instruct each child in the following procedures:

◆ Fold wrapping paper in half lengthwise.

◆ Unfold wrapping paper. Make a light pencil mark on fold line, 8 inches (20 cm) from edge (sketch a). Crease at pencil mark as shown in sketch a.

◆ Refold wrapping paper lengthwise. Cut paper as shown in sketch b to make a kite shape.

◆ Open kite. Tape long dowel or "spine" lengthwise along center fold. Tape shorter dowel or "spar" along other fold, between "wing tips" (sketch c).

◆ Use pencil to make four small holes near where dowels intersect (sketch d). Thread string through holes in criss-cross manner and tie in a knot to secure (sketch d).

◆ Wrap remaining string or "flying line" around toilet paper tube or wood scrap to make a kite reel.

◆ Tie plastic bag strips together to make a long kite tail (sketch e). Tape tail to bottom of spine.

◆ To fly kite: Take kite outside and hold it up. As wind begins to carry kite, slowly release string so kite rises with the wind.

Enrichment Idea: Decorate kite reel.

Family Talk:

Flying kites is a fun activity to do with your family. You can fly big fancy kites or use this homemade one! Do you think it's possible to have a fun family time without spending a lot of money? Yes! What fun and inexpensive activities can your family do together? You can keep these activities in mind and suggest them to your parents this weekend.

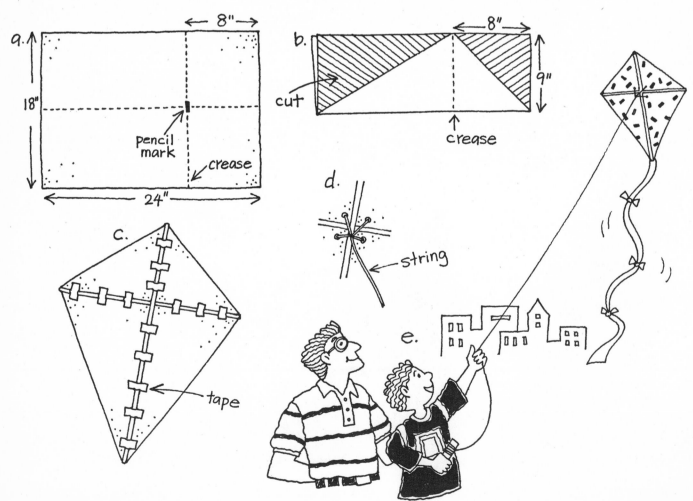

American Wind Tube

(20-25 MINUTES)

Materials: Red, white and blue construction paper; red, white and blue crepe paper streamers; string; hole punches; craft knife; glue; scissors; measuring stick. For each child—one half-gallon round ice cream container without lid.

Preparation: Use craft knife to cut bottom off of each container. Cut red and blue construction paper into 6x9-inch (15x22.5-cm) rectangles—one of each color for each child. Cut white construction paper into 2-inch (5-cm) star shapes—six for each child. Cut additional white construction paper into 1x6-inch (2.5x15-cm) strips—two for each child. Cut remainder of white construction paper into 1x16-inch (2.5x40-cm) strips—one for each child. Cut streamers into 2-foot (.6-m) lengths—four for each child. Cut string into 2-foot (.6-m) lengths—four for each child.

Instruct each child in the following procedures:

✦ Glue red construction paper onto half of container. Glue blue construction paper onto other half of container (sketch a). Overlap edges.

✦ Glue short white strips onto container to cover overlapping edges (sketch b).

✦ Glue one end of each streamer onto bottom edge of wind tube (sketch c).

✦ Glue long white strip onto wind tube to cover bottom edge (sketch d).

✦ Glue stars randomly onto wind tube to decorate.

✦ Punch four evenly spaced holes directly under top rim of container (sketch e).

✦ Tie one length of string through each hole (sketch e).

✦ Gather loose ends of string together and tie ends in a knot. Tie a knot halfway down the length of strings (sketch f).

✦ Tie wind tube to pole or porch railing for decoration. When wind blows, wind tube will float in the air.

Simplification Ideas: Cover container with one large piece of construction paper or use acrylic paint. Use silver or gold self-adhesive stars instead of cutting from construction paper.

Enrichment Idea: Older children may measure and cut their own paper, streamers and string. Provide construction paper in a variety of colors and allow children to decorate container. Tube can be decorated to commemorate any flag.

Family Talk:

What popular holiday do Americans celebrate in July? The Fourth of July celebrates freedom in America. Does your family celebrate the Fourth of July? What do you do to celebrate? Many people hang the American flag in front of their houses to show respect for their country. What other ways can we show respect for our country? Our families?

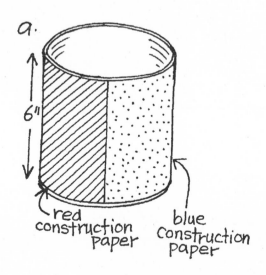

a.

6"

red construction paper

blue construction paper

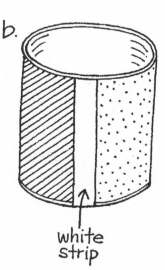

b.

white strip

(Sketches continued on page 52.)

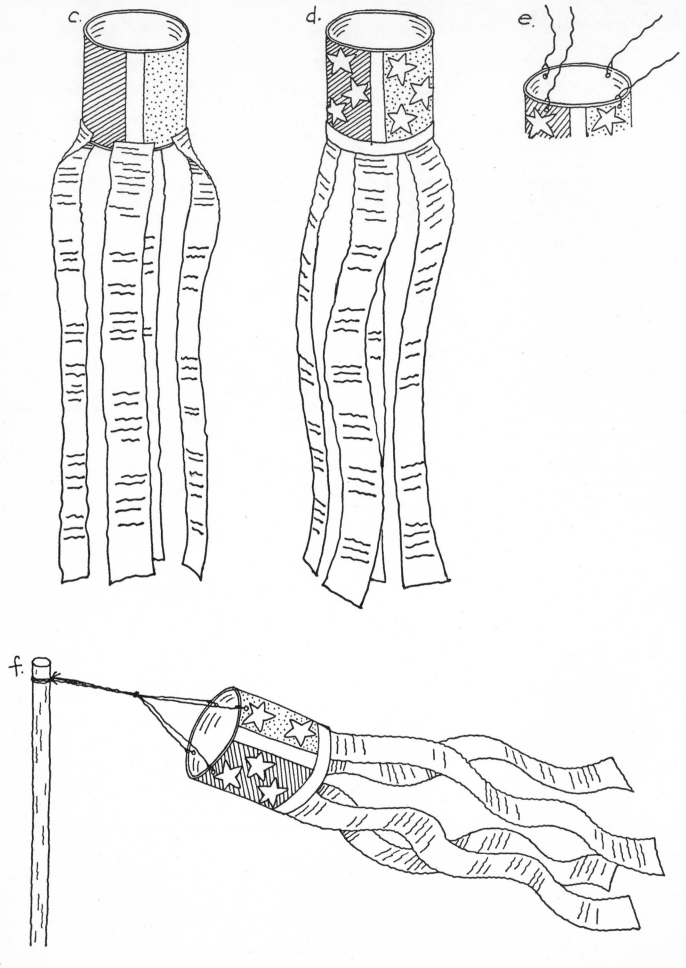

c.

d.

e.

f.

Japanese Wind Sock

(50-60 MINUTES)

Materials: Tempera paint in a variety of bright colors, paintbrushes, shallow containers, white butcher paper, pencils, black permanent felt pens, fishing line, craft knife, transparent tape, glue, scissors, rulers, measuring stick, newspaper. For each child—one plastic lid (from small coffee can or small margarine tub).

Preparation: Cut butcher paper into 16x24-inch (40x60-cm) rectangles—one for each child. Cut out center of each plastic lid to make a rim (sketch a). Cut fishing line into 15-inch (37.5-cm) lengths and 30-inch (75-cm) lengths—one of each length for each child. Fold butcher paper in half lengthwise and draw a fish shape as shown in sketch b—one for each child. Cover work area with newspaper. Pour paint into shallow containers.

Instruct each child in the following procedures:

◆ Cut out fish shape from folded paper.

◆ Unfold paper. Use pencil to sketch details on fish such as scales, eyes and fins.

◆ Paint fish and allow to dry.

◆ Use black felt pen to outline details on fish.

◆ Turn fish over, painted side down, and fold mouth opening down 1 inch (2.5 cm). Squeeze a line of glue along folded area (sketch c).

◆ Insert plastic rim inside folded area and fold paper around rim. Hold in place until glue dries.

◆ Glue seams of fish together.

◆ Fold a small piece of tape over each side of rim to reinforce fish's mouth (sketch d).

◆ Use tip of scissors to poke a small hole through each piece of tape.

◆ Tie ends of shorter length of fishing line through holes to make a bridle. Tie one end of longer length of fishing line to the midpoint of bridle (sketch d).

◆ Tie wind sock to pole or porch railing for decoration. When wind blows, wind sock will fill up with air and float horizontally.

Simplification Idea: Use felt pens or crayons instead of tempera paint.

Enrichment Ideas: Children draw their own fish or other kinds of animals. To make a longer lasting wind sock, use white fabric instead of paper.

Family Talk:

The Japanese often make wind socks in the shape of one of their favorite fishes—the carp. Do you know anybody from Japan? Optional: Show Japan on a map. **The Japanese display their wind socks each year during a festival called "Children's Day." The carp is a Japanese symbol of strength, courage and determination. What animal would you choose to describe yourself? Your family?**

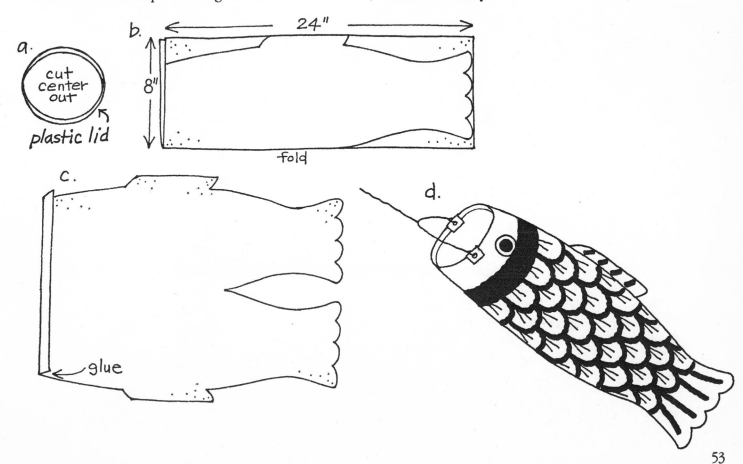

a. cut center out — plastic lid

b. 24" — 8" — fold

c. glue

d.

Jumping Jack

(45-50 MINUTES)

Materials: Body Pattern, white poster board, drill, ⅛-inch (.31-cm) drill bit, cotton string, felt pens in a variety of colors, pencils, transparent tape, scissors, ruler. For each child—four tongue depressors.

Preparation: Trace Body Pattern onto poster board and cut out—one for each child. Use drill to make five holes in poster board as shown on the pattern. Drill a hole about ¾-inch (1.9-cm) from one end of each tongue depressor (sketch a). Cut string into 5-inch (12.5-cm) lengths—three for each child. Cut additional string into 10-inch (25-cm) lengths—one for each child.

Instruct each child in the following procedures:

◆ Use felt pens to draw a head and body on poster board cutout.

◆ Color two tongue depressors to look like arms and two to look like legs (sketch a). Draw hands and feet at opposite ends of drilled holes.

◆ Wrap a piece of tape around one end of each length of string. Thread shorter length of string through body and arms as shown in sketch b. Tie knots on both ends of string at front of body. Repeat process to attach legs to body.

◆ Thread other short length of string through hole at top of head and make a loop for holding (sketch c).

◆ Tie longer length of string to the other strings as shown in sketch c.

◆ In one hand, hold figure by loop. With other hand, pull on string below to make figure jump into action!

Family Talk:

In England, Germany and other European countries, these toys are called "Jumping Jacks." What were your favorite toys when you were younger? Is there a family member you would like to give your Jumping Jack to?

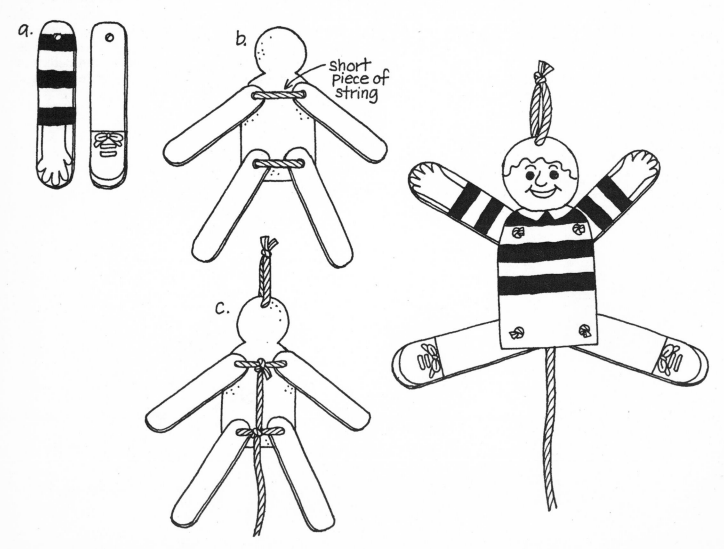

a.

b. short piece of string

c.

Jumping Jack Body Pattern

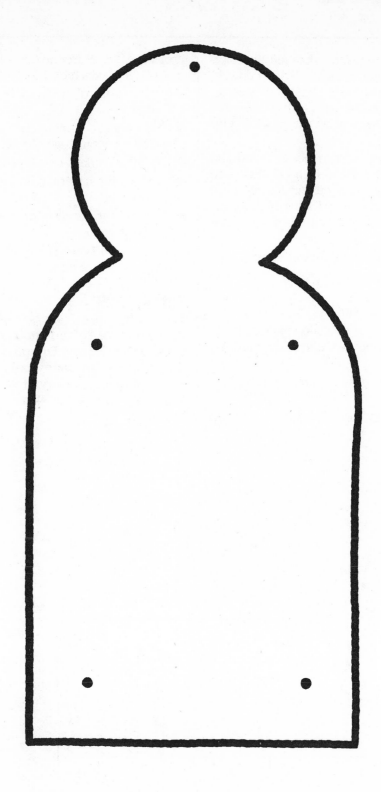

Puppet-on-a-Stick

(35-45 MINUTES)

Materials: Neck Pattern, poster board, white muslin, colorful fabric in a variety of patterns, ¼-inch (.625-cm) dowels, saw, fabric markers or permanent felt pens, yarn, pencils, transparent tape, fabric glue, scissors, ruler. For each child—one toilet paper tube, one 1½-inch (3.75-cm) Styrofoam ball.

Preparation: Trace Neck Pattern onto poster board and cut out several patterns. Draw a 4½x6-inch (11.25x15-cm) rectangle onto poster board and cut out several rectangle patterns. Cut muslin into 5½-inch (13.75-cm) circles—one for each child. Saw dowels into 12-inch (.3-m) lengths—one for each child.

Instruct each child in the following procedures:

✦ Trace Neck Pattern and rectangle pattern onto fabric and cut out.

✦ Insert end of dowel into Styrofoam ball.

✦ Cover ball with muslin circle to make puppet head. Twist edges around dowel and secure in place with tape (sketch a).

✦ Glue neck piece into a cone shape, with a ½-inch (1.25-cm) overlap (sketch b).

✦ Insert end of dowel through cone so head rests on top of cone. Tape around top of the cone to secure head onto neck (sketch c).

✦ Glue bottom of neck piece to outside edge of tube (sketch d).

✦ Glue rectangle fabric piece around tube (sketch d). Fold and glue bottom edge of fabric inside tube.

✦ Use fabric markers or felt pens to draw a face on muslin.

✦ Cut yarn for hair or fabric scraps for scarf. Glue onto puppet head.

✦ Use dowel to move puppet head up and down or hide inside tube.

Simplification Idea: For younger children, cut out all fabric pieces ahead of time.

Family Talk:

This Puppet-on-a-Stick is a popular handmade toy in the country of Poland and some other European countries. Optional: Show Europe on a map. **Europe is a continent. There are many countries in Europe—Poland is one of them. Are any of your relatives from Poland? England? Germany? Who else do you know from Europe?**

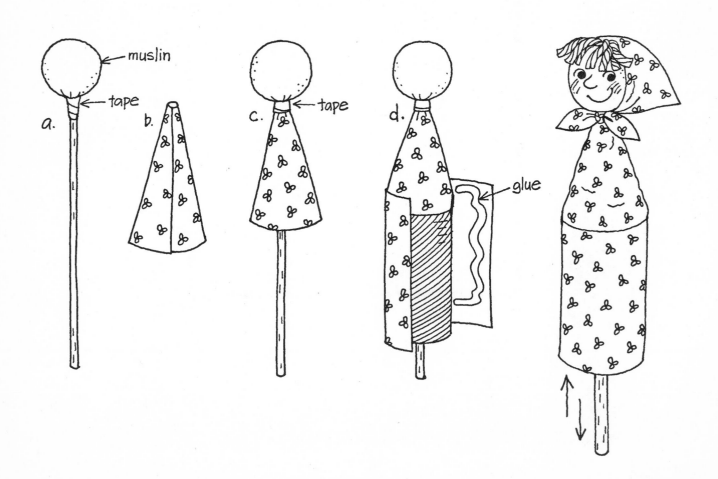

Puppet-on-a-Stick Neck Pattern

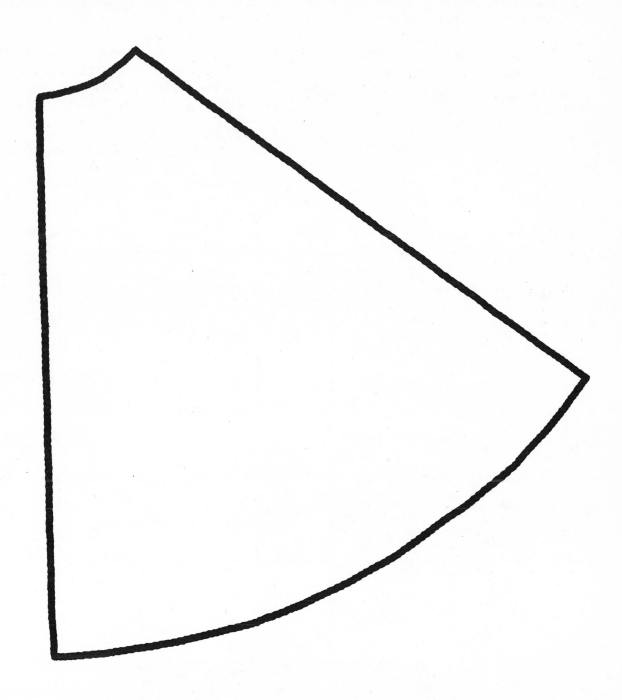

Mola Picture

(25-30 MINUTES)

Materials: Pencils, glue, craft knives or scissors with pointed tips. For each student—four sheets of 9x12-inch (22.5x30-cm) construction paper in four different colors.

Instruct each child in the following procedures:

◆ Choose four different colors of construction paper.

◆ Draw a simple outline of your house on first sheet of paper (sketch a).

◆ Carefully cut out shape of outline (shaded area on sketch).

◆ Lay first sheet of paper on top of second sheet of paper. Draw another outline about ¼-inch (.625-cm) in from the first (sketch b).

◆ Carefully cut out shape of outline from second sheet of paper.

◆ Lay second sheet on top of third sheet. Use pencil to draw a few simple details of your house (sketch c).

◆ Carefully cut out details from third sheet of paper.

◆ Glue the three cut sheets of paper together, and then glue them onto the fourth sheet of paper (sketch d).

Enrichment Idea: Mount completed picture onto a 12x18-inch (30x45-cm) sheet of black construction paper. Letter a Bible verse on a small sheet of construction paper and glue to black paper as well (see sketch).

Family Talk:

In Panama, these pictures are called *molas*. The Cuna Indians there make their molas out of brightly colored fabric. Panama is a small country in Central America. Optional: Show Panama on map. **Do any of your relatives come from or live in Central America? South America? Has any family member ever visited any countries in South America?**

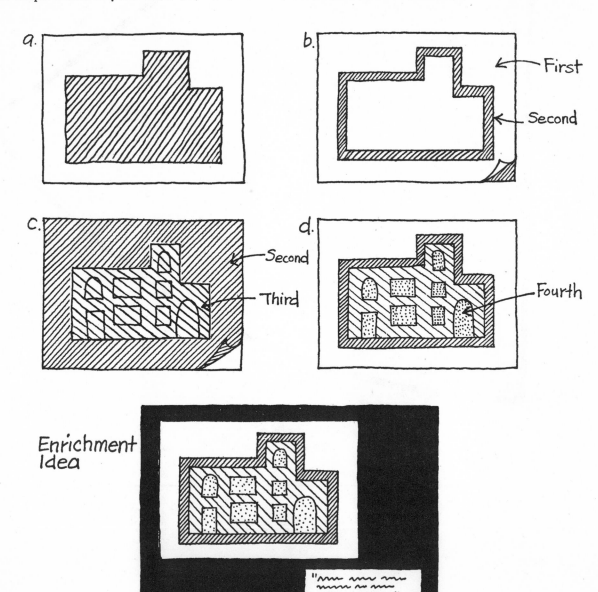

Ivy Topiary

(20-30 MINUTES)

Materials: Pliers, wire cutters, 20-gauge wire, gravel, potting soil, large spoons, measuring stick, newspaper. For each child—one 4-inch (10-cm) flower pot, one small ivy plant.

Preparation: Cut wire into 30-inch (75-cm) lengths—one for each child. Cover work area with newspaper.

Instruct each child in the following procedures:

✦ Bend one end of wire into a circle shape, smaller than the bottom of flower pot (sketch a).

✦ Bend opposite end of wire into a simple shape such as a heart, bird or star (sketch b).

✦ Place circular end of wire into bottom of pot.

✦ Cover bottom of pot with gravel.

✦ Use spoons to fill pot with potting soil.

✦ Place ivy plant in soil near wire (sketch c).

✦ Twist ivy around wire.

✦ Keep plant in a bright spot, away from direct sunlight. Water whenever soil feels dry, being careful not to over-water. As ivy grows it will continue to climb around wire shape (sketch d).

Simplification Idea: If pots are too expensive for a large group of children, plant ivy in milk cartons or tin cans.

Enrichment Idea: Use acrylic paints to decorate clay pots.

Family Talk:

Topiary plants are plants cut or formed into familiar shapes or objects. Where will you put your Ivy Topiary? What other kinds of plants do you have at home? What can you do to take care of your plants? In what ways are plants like people? If you take care of a plant it will be healthy and grow. God gave each of us a family to take care of us so that we will be healthy, too. Let's thank God for giving us families to take care of us.

Clatter Blocks

(20-30 MINUTES)

Materials: Thin plywood, saw, sandpaper, twill tape (available at fabric stores), hot glue gun and glue sticks or staple gun and staples, scissors, measuring stick.

Preparation: Saw wood into 2½x3½-inch (6.25x8.75-cm) blocks—seven for each child. Cut twill tape into 28½-inch (71.25-cm) lengths—two for each child. Cut additional twill tape into 21½-inch (53.75-cm) lengths—one for each child.

Instruct each child in the following procedures:

✦ Use sandpaper to smooth rough edges on blocks.

✦ Lay long pieces of twill tape parallel to each other, about ¾ inch (1.9 cm) apart. Glue or staple ends of tape onto blocks at both ends (sketch a).

✦ Place remaining blocks between end blocks. Alternate blocks over and under tape as shown in sketch b.

✦ Weave the shorter length of tape through blocks as shown in sketch b. Glue or staple ends of tape onto inner sides of end blocks.

✦ Hold Clatter Blocks vertically by the end block. Then grasp the second block and let the first block fall. This action should cause the other wood pieces to fall in succession.

Enrichment Idea: Stain or paint blocks with acrylic paint. Spray with clear acrylic spray before attaching twill tape.

Family Talk:

Another name for these Clatter Blocks is "Jacob's Ladder." Why do you think it is called "Jacob's Ladder"? Your Clatter Blocks are like a puzzle that takes time to figure out. Some of the most important things in life take awhile to understand. For instance, it's not always easy to understand why God lets bad things happen to us or our families, but if we keep reading the Bible and talking to Him we will grow to understand His ways more and more.

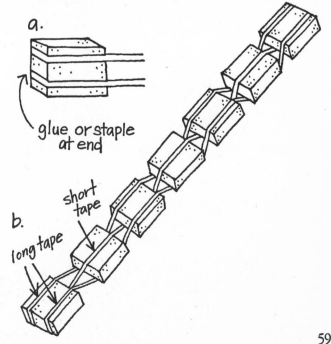

Quickie Piñata

Materials: Tissue paper in a variety of bright colors, yarn, hole punch, glue, scissors, measuring stick. For each child—one large paper grocery sack.

Preparation: Cut tissue paper into 3-inch (7.5-cm) wide strips. Cut yarn into 6-foot (1.8-m) lengths—one for each child.

Instruct each child in the following procedures:

✦ Fold down top edge of bag (sketch a).

✦ Cut slits along bottom edge of each tissue paper strip to make fringe (sketch b).

✦ Glue top edge of strip around bottom of sack (sketch c).

✦ Overlap and glue fringe of next strip to cover glued area of previous strip. Glue additional rows onto sack until entire sack is covered (sketch d).

✦ Punch holes about 2 inches (5 cm) apart along top edge of bag.

✦ Weave length of yarn through holes (sketch d).

✦ Take piñata home and fill with individually wrapped candies and small toys. Pull ends of yarn to gather top of piñata. To use piñata: Tie yarn to the branch of a tree. Blindfold a friend and allow him or her to swing at piñata with a stick or rolled up newspaper. When bag breaks everyone scrambles to pick up goodies.

Family Talk:

Piñatas were first used in the country of Italy. Clay pots were filled with goodies and then broken. Italians brought their custom to Spain, and the Spanish brought the custom to Mexico. It was the Mexicans who began making piñatas from papier-mâché and decorating them with colored tissue paper. Now piñatas are used to celebrate birthdays and other special days. How do you celebrate birthdays in your family? Do you know how your family's birthday tradition was started?

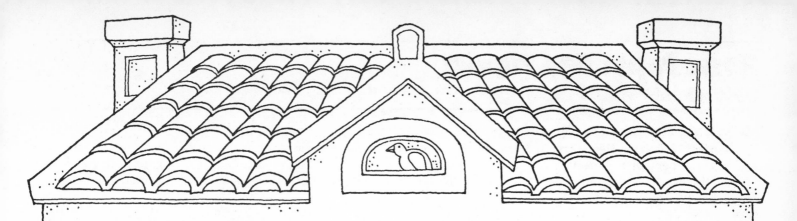

Section Four

Reproducible Pages

Bible Memory Verse Coloring Posters

The following pages are reproducible and contain 10 Bible Memory Verse designs for younger elementary children and 10 for older elementary children. Ideas for using these pages include:

1. Use the photocopied pages as awards for children who memorize the Bible verse. They may take the page home to color and display.

2. Photocopy a set of coloring posters for each student. Cover with a folded sheet of construction paper and staple to make a coloring book.

3. Use the pages in class for transition times or for students who finish an activity ahead of other students.

4. Play a coloring game. Place a variety of felt pens on the table. Recite the verse together. Then each student may choose a pen and use it to color on his or her page for one minute. When time is up, students put pens down and repeat verse together again. Students then choose another pen and color for one minute. Repeat process until pages are completed or students tire of activity.

5. To customize pages, cover the Bible verse with white paper and letter another verse or saying in its place before you photocopy.

Student Certificates and Awards

The awards and certificates on the following pages may be personalized for various uses. Just follow these simple procedures:

1. Tear out certificate and letter the name of your program on the appropriate line.

2. Photocopy as many copies of certificate as needed.

3. Letter each child's certificate with his or her name (and achievement when appropriate).

Sticker Poster

1. Photocopy a sticker poster for each student.

2. After students color posters, attach them to a wall or bulletin board.

3. Students add stickers to their posters each day as they arrive. Or you may want to use stickers as rewards for reciting Bible memory verses, being helpful, or completing assignments.

Rosie Paper Bag Puppet

(15-20 MINUTES)

Materials: A lunch-size paper bag, white card stock, photocopier, felt pens or crayons, glue, scissors.

Procedure: Photocopy Head, Arm and Leg Patterns onto card stock—two copies. Cut out one head, two arms and two legs. Use felt pens or crayons to color cutouts. Glue head to flap of paper bag as shown in sketch a. To form feet and knees, fold legs on broken lines indicated on pattern. Glue top of arms to sides of bag. Glue top of legs onto lower edge. Draw clothing details on bag as shown in sketch.

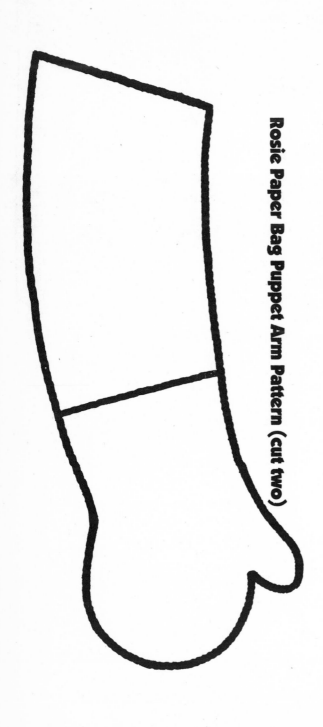

Rosie Paper Bag Puppet Arm Pattern (cut two)

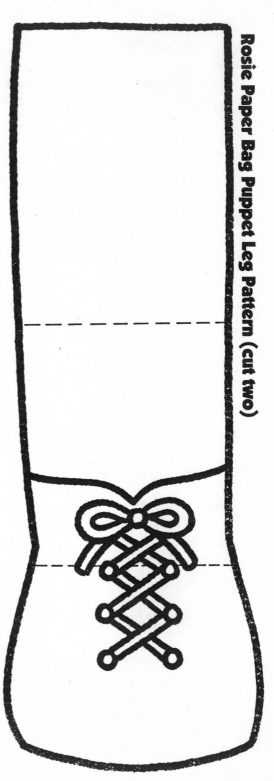

Rosie Paper Bag Puppet Leg Pattern (cut two)

Rosie Paper Bag Puppet Head Pattern

Rosie Sock Puppet

(30-45 MINUTES)

Materials: Tube sock, 3-inch (7.5-cm) Styrofoam ball, toilet paper tube, plastic sandwich bag, rubber band, felt pen, glue, scissors, pencil. For facial features—medium-sized pom-pom, large wiggle eyes, black yarn, felt and fabric scraps, ribbon.

Procedure:

✦ Cut toilet paper tube into a 2-inch (5-cm) length.

✦ Spread glue around top edge of tube and gently insert into Styrofoam ball (sketch a). This forms the neck of puppet.

✦ Place ball and tube in plastic bag and insert into sock. Slide ball to the end of sock. Secure rubber band around neck of puppet (sketch b).

✦ Insert hand into sock and place index finger in tube. Make a pencil mark on the outside of sock at location of thumb and middle finger (sketch c).

✦ Remove hand from sock and cut small finger holes at pencil marks on each side of puppet (sketch c). If edges of hole begin to unravel, spread glue along raw edges.

✦ For nose: Glue pom-pom onto front of head (sketch d).

✦ For eyes: Glue wiggle eyes onto front of head (sketch d).

✦ For mouth: Cut felt into shape of mouth and cheeks. Glue onto front of head (sketch d).

✦ For hair: Cut yarn into 24-inch (60-cm) lengths (approximately 50 strands). Tie yarn in the middle of the length (sketch e). Spread yarn so wig covers sides and back of head and glue in place. Once glue has dried, braid hair and use ribbon to secure braid (sketch f).

✦ For clothes: Glue scrap of fabric around shoulders to make a shawl (sketch g).

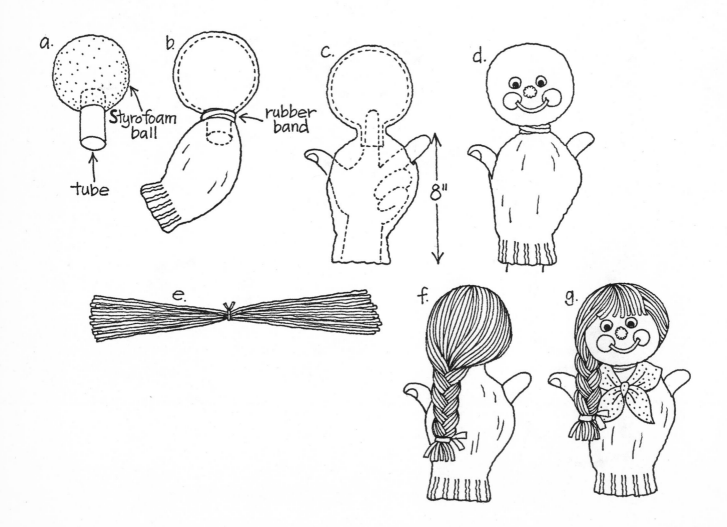

Mrs. Pumpernic Bagel Shop

LEE'S MARKET

"Honor your father and your mother,
as the Lord your God has commanded you."
Deuteronomy 5:16

"Forgive as the Lord forgave you."
Colossians 3:13

Joe's Ice Cream

"Let love and faithfulness never leave you."
Proverbs 3:3

Younger Elementary Coloring Page 3

"Be quick to listen, slow to speak and slow to become angry."

James 1:19

"How great is the love the Father has lavished on us,
that we should be called children of God!"
1 John 3:1

FATHER

HONOR

MOTHER

STOP

Beauty Shop

BUS

"Your father and your mother, as the Lord Your God has commanded you." Deuteronomy 5:16

Older Elementary Coloring Page 1

LORD 4GIVES US OTHERS

"Bear with each other and forgive whatever grievances you may have against one another. Forgive as the Lord forgave you."

Colossians 3:13

"Let love and faithfulness never leave you;...
write them on the tablet of your heart."
Proverbs 3:3

Finish

Everyone should be quick to listen, slow to speak and slow to become angry." James 1:19

Start

Start

"How great is the love the Father has lavished on us, that we should be called children of God!"

1 John 3:1

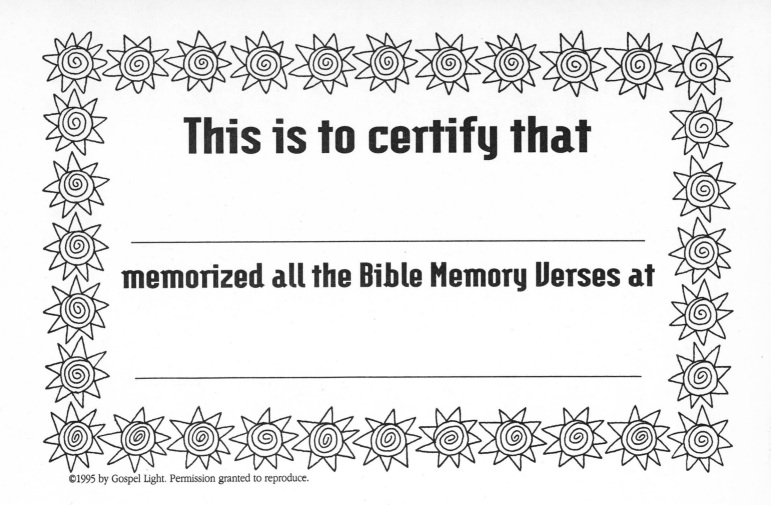

This is to certify that

_____

memorized all the Bible Memory Verses at

_____

_____

thanks for being part of our family at

_____

Good Neighbor Award

_____

was a good friend at

_____

VISITOR AWARD
we're glad you joined us at

_____

**PLEASE COME
BACK AGAIN!**

Welcome!

_____

thanks for being a community helper

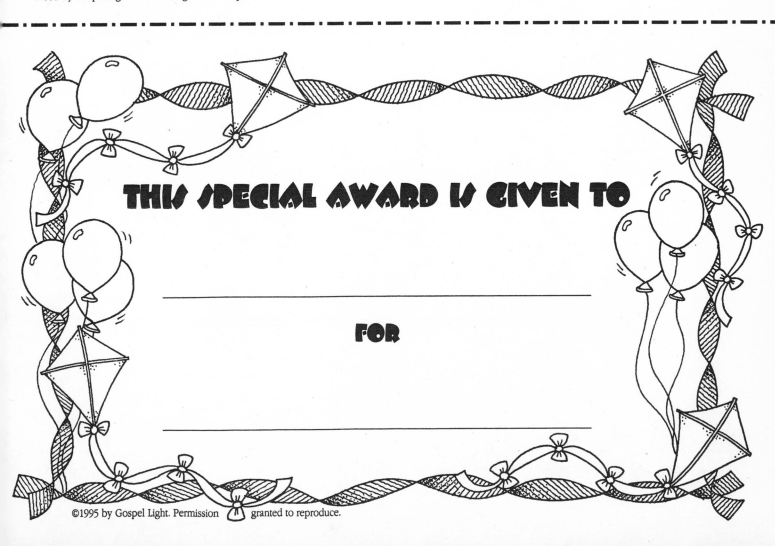

THIS SPECIAL AWARD IS GIVEN TO

_____

FOR

_____

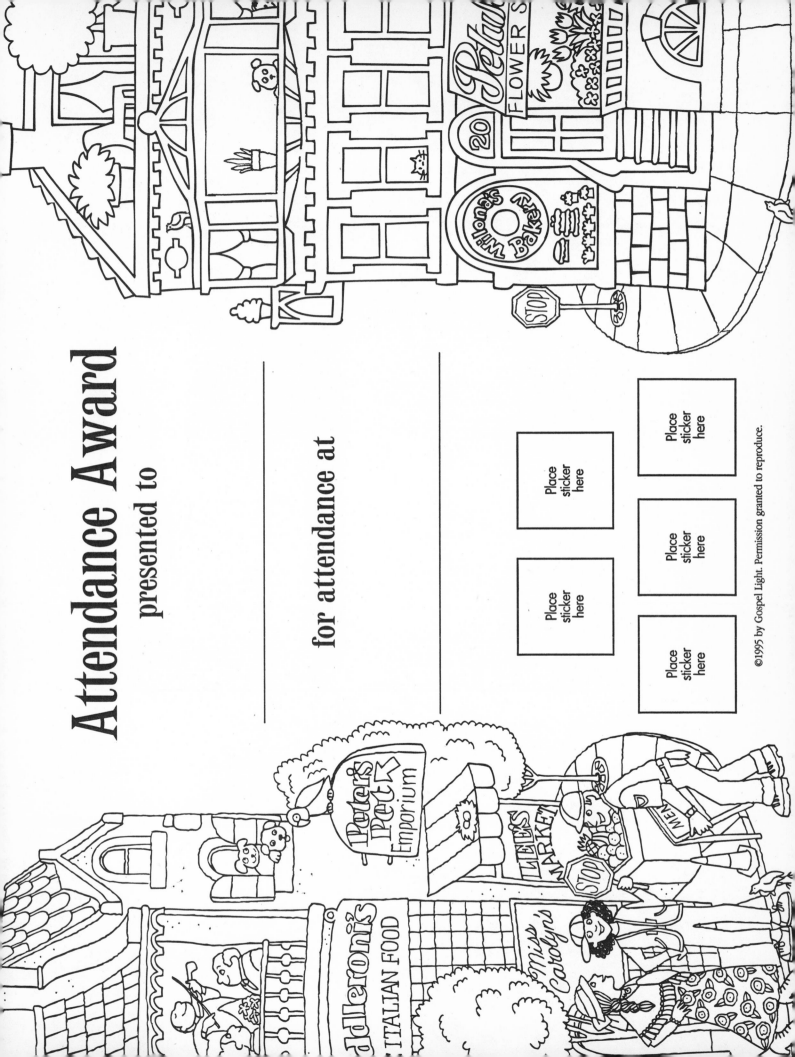

Attendance Award

presented to

for attendance at

Place sticker here

Place sticker here

Place sticker here

Place sticker here

Place sticker here

©1995 by Gospel Light. Permission granted to reproduce.

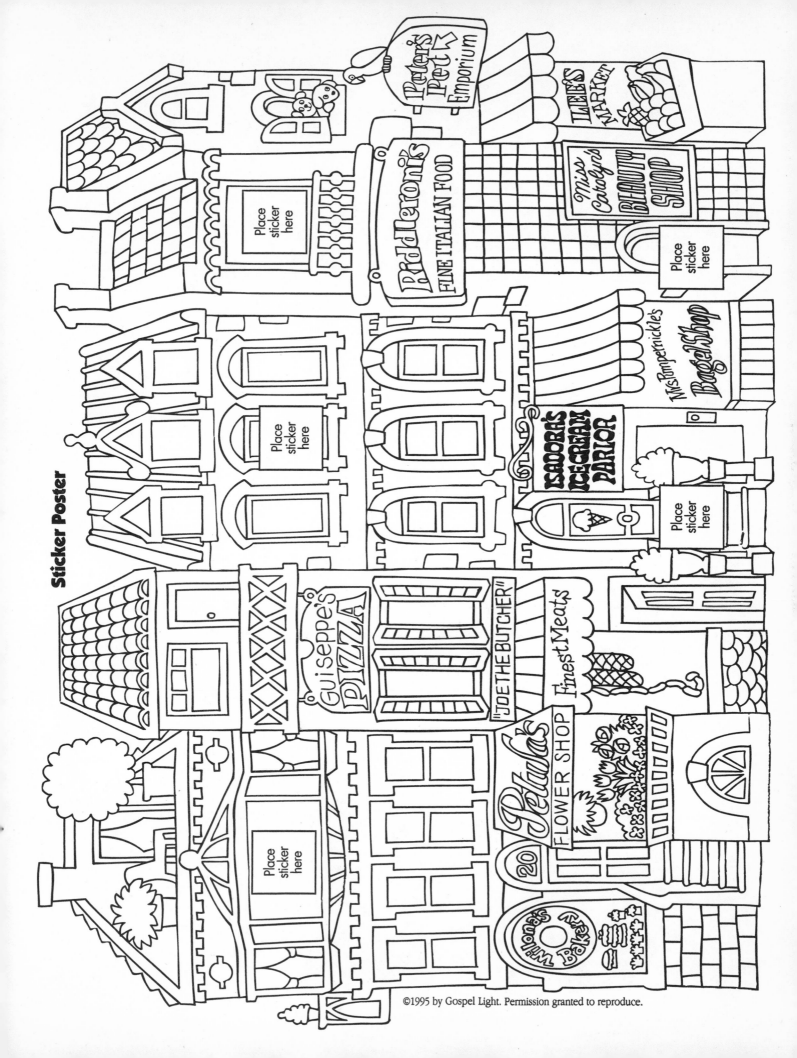

Sticker Poster

Peter's Pet Emporium

LEE'S MARKET

Miss Carolyn's BEAUTY SHOP

Riddleroni's FINE ITALIAN FOOD

Place sticker here

Place sticker here

Mrs. Pompetrickle's Bagel Shop

Place sticker here

ISADORA'S ICECREAM PARLOR

Place sticker here

Guiseppe's PIZZA

"JOE THE BUTCHER" Finest Meats

Petula's FLOWER SHOP

20

Wilona's Bakery

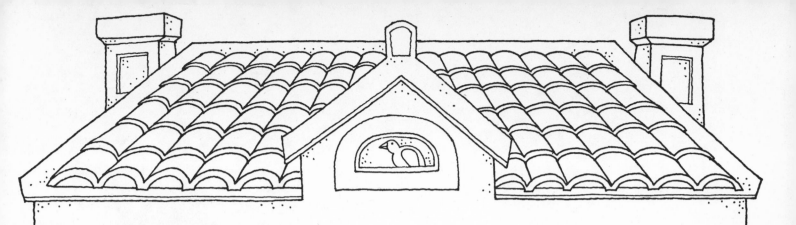

Index